THE CROSS
The Dividing Line

Daudu Emmanuel Solomon

ISBN: 9798844255960

DEDICATION

This Book is Dedicated to God, to my Family, and to people of the World.

CONTENTS

INTRODUCTION

We live in a world that is continually becoming hostile to God and the things of God: the trends, the movies, the school and organizations. Most of this attacks is against Christianity and the Gospel. And so many times because of the pressures of the world, Christians have come to start to doubt their fate and doubt the validity of the Bible. These pressures are not external alone, they can also come from the church itself with false doctrines, false prophets and everyone doing things like the Church was theirs instead of Christ's.

This book is designed to bring you back into perspective, to restore your trust in God and His word by showing you His manifold Wisdom and how He placed it in His word in types, in symbols and in Prophecy: With hundreds to thousands of years of fulfilment hence proving the Divinity of the Bible.

THE Bible is a textbook of One person, Jesus Christ. The Old Testament (The Law Psalm, the Songs and the Prophet) all depict Him. The Divine creativity, wisdom, Accuracy proves that it was inspired and written by God; the author.

From the beginning of the "Let there be Light" of Genesis to the "Amen" of Revelation depicts Jesus Christ.

Luke 24:44 "Then Jesus said to them, this is what I told

you while I was still with you, everything which is written concerning Me in the Law of Moses the Prophets and the Psalms must be fulfilled".

This book is going to touch on several important areas, as it gives lessons, secrets, instructions, patterns and warning and pointing out Jesus every step of the way.

Let it take you through this Journey and Trust God to give understanding.

1 THE BEGINNING

Jesus is the Centrality of the Bible, it was written to show us Christ, His assignment and how it was fulfilled on the Cross and His Heavenly ministry.

I'll start with the very beginning of the let there be Light.

Genesis 1:2-3[2]And the earth was without form, and void; and darkness was upon the face of the deep. And the Spirit of God moved upon the face of the waters.[3]And God said, LET THERE BE LIGHT and there was light.

That's odd because the Sun and moon was actually created from verse 14 of Genesis

Genesis 1:14 [14]And God said, Let there be lights in the firmament of the heaven to divide the day from the night; and let them be for signs, and for seasons, and for days, and years:

So what is this Light?

John 8:12 Then spoke Jesus to them, saying, I AM THE LIGHT OF THE World: he that followeth me shall not walk in darkness, but shall have the light of life.

John 1:4,9 [4]In him (JESUS) was life; and the life was the LIGHT of men.[9]That(referring to Jesus) was the TRUE LIGHT which lighteth every man that cometh into the world.

JESUS IS THE TRUE LIGHT

John 1:1 "In the beginning was the word, and the word was with God and Word was God Himself".

From the first time that God use the word "let there be light" that was Jesus.

A more mind blowing symbol which is getting popular is in Genesis which talks about the genealogy of Noah from Adam.

- Adam begat Seth
- Seth begat Enosh
- Enosh begat Kenan
- Kenan begat Mahalalel
- Mahalalel begat Jared
- Jared begat Enoch
- Enoch begat Methuselah
- Methuselah begat Lamech
- Lamech begat Noah

This is a very interesting symbol of Jesus of the Gospel of God's plan of redemption

- Adam means man
- Seth means appointed or (acquired)

- Enosh means miserable
- Kenan means sorrow
- Mahalalel means the blessed God or the gift of God
- Jared means shall come down
- Enosh means teaching
- Methuselah means His death shall bring
- Lamech means despairing
- Noah means rest

Putting the means together we read a beautiful story about a person. "Man acquired miserable sorrow but the blessed God will come down teaching and His death shall bring the despairing rest"

The Beginning of Sorrows

When God was pronouncing judgement on the devil.

Genesis 3:15[15]And I will put enmity between thee and the woman, and between thy seed and her seed; it shall bruise thy head, and thou shalt bruise his heel.

The word "seed" (singular, definite) referring to the person of Jesus.

Biologically, women do not have seed (in the context of sperm for child bearing) but men do.

For a woman to have seed, it has to be implanted (speaking of the virgin birth of Jesus Christ). When God made this statement to the devil, the devil started hunting that seed.

Firstly since God accepted Abel's sacrifice (which was to symbolize the sacrifice of Jesus on the Cross), the devil used Cain to kill Abel. Because he thought Abel was that promised "seed of the woman" who was to bruise his head. Even Eve thought she acquired that "Seed" through her third Son "Seth" which means "Acquired".

When Adam sinned, the sin nature entered into him, entered into his life. Sin entered into our blood line and if Jesus who was to redeem man had been born in the normal way, He too would have the sin nature; how can a prisoner set another prisoner free?

It has been scientifically proven that when a child is in the womb, its mother's blood has nothing to do with the child. Everything is supplied from the seed; the mother just houses and feeds the Child which is not an easy task by the way.

Jesus didn't have the sin nature at all that's why He was very qualified to take our sins and be as a means of exchange; a substitute for us.

There was a reason God sent man out of the garden and prevented him from eating from the Tree of Life after Adam sinned: Many of us just think God was angry that's all but the truth is that God actually did man a favour. If Adam had eaten from the Tree of Life after he sinned, then God and man would never come to terms; we would eternally be separated from God. That's why even when Adam sinned God was proclaiming

Jesus His Son in other words, God was the first to preach the Gospel to man. And after that encounter, God killed a Ram and clothed Adam with it. We would come to the significance of the sacrifice of Ram later on in this book.

When God put Adam in the garden, He gave Adam a choice and was warned. God did not create a Robot and keep it in the garden.

The tree of life was in the garden and God said "eat of every tree in the garden" including the Tree of life. If Adam had eaten the tree of life signifying the life of God before he fell, then he wouldn't have even had the chance to fall at all because even though he was made in the image of God and crowned with God's glory, He did not have the life of God. God gave Adam a choice but he made a horrible decision that has brought mankind to a terrible state. Satan (sin) has destroyed everything. God wanted good for mankind. He created everything man would ever need first before creating man.

God created the heavens and the earth and made man in charge of the earth. God gave man dominion over the earth in order words man was the god of the earth.

Psalms 115:16[16]The heaven, even the heavens, are the LORD'S: but the earth hath he given to the children of men.

Satan was envious of Adam because God gave man so much favour and authority. Adam was to represent and express God on earth.

The devil could not come directly to Adam because. Adam had the power to rubbish him. Instead, the devil came as a cunning serpent with stealth deceived man, man fell and man lost everything.

God's judgement was now hanging on man, the sin nature became a part of man's existence and God cannot relate with sinful men even if he wanted to. Since Mankind was now in Sin, if God should judge Sin then by default, He judges man. He can't judge one as exclude the other if He is to be a perfect Judge. So God had to look for a way to separate Man from Sin so that He could Judge sin eternally and not Judge Man.

God is just judge let me give an instance; if you are a judge and your best friend or relative commits a heinous crime and you were the presiding judge in that case though you love your best friend or relative you still have to do the right thing and sentence him/her.

Even though God loved man, God's judgement was still hanging on man that's why Jesus came to die on the cross (death was pronounced on Adam) for our sin, Jesus absorbed all God's righteous judgement on our behalf. When Adam sinned, Satan had the legal right to cause all sorts of pain to man, disasters, diseases, death, wars etc. Satan became the god of this world, truncating Adam: this became the beginning of sorrows and everything horrible in the world. Anything that Satan is god of turns into a disaster heading to even more disaster.

The Sin issue had so much effect that it also affected creation. Creation fell too.

God is now on a rescue mission to save man and to reclaim His absolute dominion over the earth.

God wanted man to rule the earth He had created. In a sense having absolute dominion but through man. God created man in His own image and Likeness so that through Adam, God could have Children in His own image and Likeness. But as Adam sinned and took on the sin Nature, Adam and the rest of mankind became perverted. Instead of giving birth to Children in the image and Likeness of God, Adam gave birth to Children in his own perverted image and Likeness.

In order to redeem mankind, God needs to recreate man through the second Adam(Jesus Christ) so that by believing in Jesus sacrifice, God can now have the Children He intended (and the totality of that will be gotten at His second coming).

2 THE ARK OF NOAH AND THE REBELLIOUS WORLD

These days, Atheism has begin to spread exponentially, we thought it was only in Western countries but it has actually come much closer.

I believe that some of us have actually questioned the concept of God at a point (welcome to the club), maybe because of situations and culture.

God works with patterns, if you search well; what will happen in the future has the same pattern of what has happened in the past but under very different circumstances.

In the days of Noah, when Noah preached about the coming judgement of God and that the ark was the only means of escape, he was ridiculed and they all thought he was crazy until the Judgement came and it was too late. That is the same thing happening in our world, the concept of God is censored or laughed at especially in regards to the Gospel.

Jesus is the ark now that will shield you from the coming Judgement and also oppression from Satan. Unfortunately the past will repeat itself for millions of people. Don't let it be you

All of mankind inherited Adam's transgression and Satan's nature. If God should judge Satan, He also has to judge those with Satan's nature. But praise be to God that through Jesus, this nature is wiped out and a new nature is born. A nature that's in the world but not of the world.

2 Corinthians 5:17[17]Therefore if any man be in Christ, he is a new creature: old things are passed away; behold, all things are become new.

Methuselah's story is a very unique one, the name Methuselah means "His death shall bring". God pronounced judgement on the earth because of their grievous sins. But God gave them hundreds of years to repent. According to Hebrew Targums; When Methuselah was born, God pronounced that His judgement would come when Methuselah dies. After hundreds of years Noah was born and God told Noah about the judgement that was coming soon. God told Noah to build an Ark. Noah told the people about God's coming judgement but they made light of it.

Genesis 6:9-14[9]These are the generations of Noah: Noah was a just man and perfect in his generations, and Noah walked with God.[10]And Noah begat three sons,

Shem, Ham, and Japheth.[11]The earth also was corrupt before God, and the earth was filled with violence.[12]And God looked upon the earth, and, behold, it was corrupt; for all flesh had corrupted his way upon the earth.[13]And God said unto Noah, The end of all flesh is come before me; for the earth is filled with violence through them; and, behold, I will destroy them with the earth.[14]Make thee an ark of gopher wood; rooms shalt thou make in the ark, and shalt pitch it within and without with pitch.

Noah was going about telling people about God's coming judgement and that the Ark will save them from it.

2 Peter 2:5[5]And spared not the old world, but saved Noah the eighth person, a preacher of righteousness, bringing in the flood upon the world of the ungodly;

Noah a preacher who was telling the world about God's judgement and entering the Ark was the only way to be saved; which is symbolic of Jesus death that saved us from God's judgement.

But they did not heed Noah's word.

1 Peter 3:20[20]Which sometime were disobedient, when once the long-suffering of God waited in the days of Noah, while the ark was a preparing, wherein few, that is, eight souls were saved by water.

After God said that "His judgement will come on the wicked world when Methuselah dies," God in His great mercies made Methuselah to live up to 969 years for the people to change from their wicked ways; but they ignored Him. Just as it is in our modern world, God has given us a chance to avoid eternal judgement through the death of His son (so that we could believe and be saved) but many are rejecting that simple call.

Noah finished building the Ark and one week after Methuselah's death, the flood began. Noah and His seven (7) other relatives entered the Ark and God shut them inside. Even though God's judgement through the flood came fiercely, killing those people of old, Noah and his family were safe. God's judgement battered the Ark through the waves of the flood but Noah and his families were safe. The ark was just a symbol but the reality is Jesus Christ. Those who are in Christ Jesus have been free from eternal judgement because God battered Jesus His son on the cross with His judgement.

Despite the waves, the Ark stood intact. It took on all the waves of God's judgement regarding sin, Jesus took upon Himself all of God's judgement for us.

3 THE CALLED RACE

Before we see how this symbolizes what Jesus will do on the Cross, It's important to note some important biblical facts you may have been missing

Abraham

God called Abraham out and separated Him from his family instructing him to go to Bethel in Canaan and dwell there, Abraham eventually decided to leave there and went down to Egypt.

Genesis 12:8-10[8]And he removed from thence unto a mountain on the east of Bethel, and pitched his tent, having Bethel on the west, and Hai on the east: and there he built an altar unto the LORD, and called upon the name of the LORD.[9]And Abram journeyed, going on still toward the south.[10]And there was a famine in the land: and Abram went down into Egypt to sojourn there; for the famine was grievous in the land.

God didn't instruct Abraham to go down to Egypt, this was Abraham's own idea. If you look closely in the Bible going anywhere that is not Jerusalem (or the promised land) is recorded as "**going down"** which is a symbol of going down from the Spirit or the Cross to the flesh,or leaving the presence of God which usually results in various problems as we see in the cases of Abraham, Isaac and Jacob. The man that had seen God became not just a coward but a liar that traded his wife Sarah to Pharoah, passing her off like his sister. And had God not intervened, the bloodline that should have brought the promised seed (Christ) would have been corrupted.

Luke10:30[30]And Jesus answering said, A certain man went Down From Jerusalem and fell among thieves, which stripped him of his raiment, and wounded him, and departed, leaving him half dead."

As Jesus gave the case with the Jew helped by the good Samaritan, the Jew **went down** from Jerusalem to Jericho and was attacked by thieves.

When Abraham was in Bethel, He built an altar (which was a picture of the cross) but when He went down to Egypt there was no mention of an altar. Immediately He left Canaan down to Egypt, His Flesh flared up and Lies followed. He lied to Pharoah put the seed at risk. At that point in Egypt, there was no communication between Abraham and God, until He went back Up to Canaan (which will later house Jerusalem)

Genesis 13:1[1]And Abram WENT UP OUT OF EGYPT, he, and his wife, and all that he had, and Lot with him, into the south.So the moment we don't focus on the cross, the flesh rises up.

Since there was no communication between God and Abraham in Egypt, he became a useless Child of God and was even rejected by the world as Pharoah sent him out because he became a plague to them. Abraham opt-in for self-help without consulting God led to all kinds of problems as we see with other great men in the Bible like Elijah, David, Samuel at some instances. Abraham didn't totally learn the lesson of not relying on self. This time he took the advice of his wife, got another woman pregnant and gave birth to Ishmael. And even today the world is still suffering and has suffered tremendous loss of lives by his descendants alone. But before we may condemn Abraham, we should look at ourselves first. We do it all the time.

Abraham And Isaac

Abraham did learn obedience and he showed it in one of the most severe scenarios. He became one of the champions of Obedience with this single act of sacrificing his son; Isaac.

Genesis 22:1-2[1]And it came to pass after these things, that God did tempt Abraham, and said unto him, Abraham: and he said, Behold, here I am.[2]And he said, Take now thy son, thine only son Isaac, whom thou lovest, and get thee into the land of Moriah; and offer him there for a burnt offering upon one of the mountains which I will tell thee of.

Abraham who waited for decades (99 years to be exact) for the promised Son Isaac is now told by God to sacrifice his Son. I can't imagine how heart wrenching that would have felt. Nevertheless Abraham set out to Obey. I believe he did not tell his wife if not, we might have been telling another story today.

Genesis 22:3-6[3]And Abraham rose up early in the morning, and saddled his ass, and took two of his young men with him, and Isaac his son, and clave the wood for the burnt offering, and rose up, and went unto the place of which God had told him.[4]Then on the third day Abraham lifted up his eyes, and saw the place afar off.[5]And Abraham said unto his young men, Abide ye here with the ass; and I and the lad will go yonder and worship, and come again to you.[6]And Abraham took the wood of the burnt offering, and laid it upon Isaac his son; and he took the fire in his hand, and a knife; and they went both of them together.

Isaac was symbolic of Jesus. Isaac carried the wood himself as Jesus carried the cross Himself. He Climbed mount Moriah the same mountain as mount Calvary where Jesus was crucified.

There was a reason why God told Abraham to climb a mountain because Abraham could have just sacrificed Isaac without climbing the mountain. So God was painting a picture of the cross. Abraham was symbolic of God how God will sacrifice His son on the cross.

Genesis 22:7-9[7]And Isaac spake unto Abraham his father, and said, My father: and he said, Here am I, my son. And he said, Behold the fire and the wood: but where is the lamb for a burnt offering?[8]And Abraham said, My son, God will provide himself a lamb for a burnt offering: so they went both of them together.[9]And they came to the place which God had told him of; and Abraham built an altar there, and laid the wood in order, and bound Isaac his son, and laid him on the altar upon the wood.

When Abraham was about to sacrifice Isaac, an Angel called to him from heaven.

Genesis 22:11-12[11]And the angel of the LORD called unto him out of heaven, and said, Abraham, Abraham: and he said, Here am I.[12]And he said, Lay not thine hand upon the lad, neither do thou any thing unto him: for now I know that thou fearest God, seeing thou hast not withheld thy son, thine only son from me.

The same person that called out Abraham Abraham was the same that called out Martha Martha, Samuel Samuel, Saul Saul. That angel was a pre-incarnate appearance of Christ. As He had appeared to Gideon, Samson's parents, Elijah (when he fled from Jezebel), the fourth man in the fire of Daniel and more.

Genesis 22:13 "Abraham looked up and saw a ram

caught by its horns in a thicket so Abraham took the lamb and offered it as a burnt offering in the place of his son."

Now the ram is symbolic for Jesus **"Abraham said God Himself will provide the Lamb"** John said this of Jesus

John 1:29 "the next day, John saw Jesus coming towards him and said, look, there is the lamb of God, who takes away the sin of the world."

The Ram was caught by its horn in a thicket.

Shepherd know that catching a Ram by its thicket is a death wish; because a Ram strength is in its horns so in a way, the Ram was picturing how Jesus though all powerful and supreme, He allowed Himself to be crucified for us

A thicket is a thorny piece of bush and like the Ram, Jesus wore a crown of thorns on His head during His crucifixion.

Jesus said to the Pharisees

John 8:56[56]Your father Abraham rejoiced to see my day: and he saw it, and was glad.

Abraham saw Jesus' day on the Mount Moriah. The whole drama of the sacrifice of Isaac showed Abraham how God will punish, sacrifice, judge His own Son for mankind; which brought gladness to Abraham. He saw that through faith in Jesus death you would be made righteous.

Hebrew 11:13 "These Abraham, Noah, Abel, Enoch, Sarah) all died in faith without having received the promises (promises of the cross) but they saw them from a distance (in Abraham case on mount Moriah, greeted them and confessed that there were foreigners and temporary residents on the earth."

So this people saw a picture of Jesus but not the reality, they saw a shadow but not the reality, they saw the advertisement, but not the goods. We now have the reality we are just ignorant of it.

The Stairways Jacob saw

Jacob was arguably the most adventurous character in the Bible, he really had a lot of drama in his Life: a lot caused by his ability to deceive. The Patriarch of Israel always wanting to accomplish the things of God with his own ability (which led to disaster) and constantly getting into trouble. However God was still with Him.

The first appearance of God to Jacob was at Bethel when he was gripped by fear because of the threat of Esau after he took the birthright and blessings. It was at one of his lowest points of Jacob's Life that the LORD appeared in a dream.

Genesis 28:12[12]And Jacob dreamed, and behold a staircase set up on the earth, and the top of it reached to heaven: and behold the angels of God ASCENDING AND DESCENDING ON IT" and God standing on it.

John 1:51 And Jesus saith unto him, Verily, verily, I say unto you, Hereafter ye shall see heaven open, and the angels of God ASCENDING AND DESCENDING upon the Son of man(Jesus Himself).

So that staircase Jacob saw was a symbol of Jesus as the only way to Heaven and to God.

Just as most prophecies were written over a thousand years prior that only Jesus could fulfill. Prophecies (especially of Jesus) gives validity to the Bible as Divine.

There are numerous prophecies written concerning Jesus, many of which was prophesied by Isaiah alone. This is one of the most important aspect of strengthening your belief in Jesus and annulling false religions, agnostics and atheists. There should be over a thousand prophecies concerning just Jesus alone. Anyways I'll be handling some of the mind blowing ones; some may look like paradoxes or juxtapositions. I'll be going in debt in the realm of Prophecy in my book "The Cross (the centrality of the universe) which will also look into how the three wise men could read about Jesus from the stars.

Joseph

Joseph is another person who played the role of Jesus Christ. Joseph was loved by Israel (Jacob) more than all his other brothers. When Joseph's brothers perceived this they hated him and could not bring themselves to speak peaceably with Him

(Genesis 37:4). Then Joseph had a dream which made the hatred grow more, the dream implied that He will rule over his brothers, his brothers were furious with him. Joseph's brothers originally devised a plan to kill Joseph but later sold Him to the Egyptians.

Joseph was falsely accused and put into a pit (prison) Joseph was the head of that pit. Joseph got out of the pit (prison) he became the ruler of Egypt later on, his brothers who sold him recognized him and wept bitterly.

Joseph came to the rescue of Israel at the time of serious famine (trouble) because of (Joseph, Israel found favour in the eyes of the Egyptian king).

Jesus was loved dearly by His Father (God) because He pleased God but Jesus brothers; the Jews (especially the Pharisees) hated Him they always cursed, insulted and mocked Jesus anytime they had the opportunity. They devised plans to put Jesus to death and handed Him to the Romans to do so. Jesus was falsely accused severally.

After that Jesus went to hell (pit) not to suffer for sin as some erroneously believe. He had already fully dealt with Sin the moment He Cried "It if Finished".

So many people don't really get the reasons why Jesus descended to hell, some ignorantly say He went to suffer for us. But everything was accomplished the time Jesus said "it is finished". If it was not finished Jesus won't say so, let me lead you to a verse

1 Peter 3:19-20 "by which also He (Jesus Christ) went and preached (proclaim) unto the spirit in prison which sometime were disobedient. When once the long-suffering (patience) of God waited in the days of Noah, while the Ark was preparing wherein few, that is, eight souls were saved by water."

In summary Jesus went to preach (proclaim the right word) to the spirits in prison during the days of Noah. I believe it is talking about those spirits that left their realm and came to sleep with the daughters of men. They are the Nephillim of Genesis 6.

Genesis 6:1-2 "and it came to pass, when men began to multiply on the face of the earth and daughters were born unto them, that the sons of God (referring to angels at this instance) saw the daughters of men they were fair (beautiful) and they took them wives of all they chose."

Jude paints a clearer picture.

Jude 1:6 "And the angels which kept not their first estate (their realm), but left their own habitation, he hath reserved in everlasting chains under darkness unto the judgement of the great day."

1 Peter 3:19 "by which also He (Jesus) went and proclaimed to the spirit in prison"

Those Fallen angels that came to earth to lay with the daughters of men in the times of Noah were trying to contaminate the seed of the woman which is Jesus. From the moment God told Satan **"the seed of the woman will bruise your head"** the devil attempted numerous ways either to stop the seed or contaminate the lineage by which that Seed of the woman would come from. The devil tried using genetics to contaminate the seed. So Jesus went to proclaim to those spirits in prison that their plan to stop Him from being born failed.

Jesus played "in your face" type of scenario to those spirits put in prison during the days of Noah who attempted to stop His incarnation as Man.

Joseph was put in prison but even in prison, he was in charge, he was the head. When Jesus descended to hell, Jesus was the head there, He was the most powerful there. When Joseph was out of prison, Joseph became the ruler in Egypt overall ruler in Egypt. Jesus now is the resurrected king the king of kings.

When Joseph's brothers realized that he was king over Israel they wept bitterly. When Jesus the king of kings come to save Israel from doom on the last day, the Jews (Jesus brothers) would recognize Him and weep bitterly.

As Joseph said "if they had not sold him to Egypt, then they would not have found redemption from the famine". Though his brothers intended bad for him, but God tuned it for good. The same way that the Jews conspired to kill Jesus which has now brought redemption from judgement for the whole world if we only believe and accept Him.

4 THE DELIVERANCE

This is recorded as one the Most Monumental events in the History of Israel: their deliverance from their over 200 years of enslavement in Egypt. God so much paid special attention to this so much that anytime He wanted to redeem, bless or instruct Israel He reminds them of Egypt.

This whole story showed us a pattern of what was truly happening to the human race under the enslavement of the devil for thousands of Years and how God will come to redeem Humanity; but not without a fight from Satan.

Pharoah symbolized Satan, Egypt signified Satan's kingdom or the world, the gods of Egypt signified demonic Spirits and Israel the Human race (at least those who would believe)

We are going to see how all these fit and other secrets and lessons and also seeing Jesus in every step of the way

The Burning Bush

This is one of the most notable miracles in the Bible. Moses was tending to his sheep as a shepherd and noticed this wonder. A bush clearly on fire but it wasn't burning. That Burning Bush was a picture of Christ, Humanity joined to Divinity. In the Bible or in Hebrew tradition, wood (or tree) was a symbol of man

Mark 8:23-24[23]And Jesus took the blind man by the hand, and led him out of the town; and when he had spit on his eyes, and put his hands upon him, he asked him if **he saw ought.[24]And he looked up, and said, I see men as trees, walking".**

Fire however, was a symbol of God; God was with Israel as a pillar of Fire, He appeared in the Temple as Fire and He came down through His Spirit on believers as a tongue of Fire.

Hebrews 12:29[29]For our God is a consuming fire.(Deuteronomy 4:24, 9:3).

Only one person in the entire world fits this description and that's Jesus Christ; God in Human Flesh.

Moses

Moses was a picture of Christ in many instances from the fact that He was a priest king and prophet, being chosen from birth to redeem Israel to the fact that he was a mediator or the old covenant (the Law). Moses was saddled with the responsibility of redeeming Israel (with God as the source) from Egypt and Pharoah just as Jesus was saddled with the responsibility of redeeming the whole of mankind from the world and Satan.

God gave Moses two signs at the burning bush.

1. The rod he was holding turning into a snake and turning back into a rod

Exodus 4:3-4[3]And he said, Cast it on the ground. And he cast it on the ground, and it became a serpent; and Moses fled from before it.[4]And the LORD said unto Moses, Put forth your hand, and take it by the tail. And he put forth his hand, and caught it, and it became a rod in his hand:

This is God telling Moses that he is going to fight against the kingdom of darkness (with the serpent being a symbol of Satan) and that he was going to win this battle.

2. The second miracle where his hand turned Leprous and then turned back to a healthy one.

Exodus 4:6-7[6]And the LORD said furthermore to him, Put your hand into your bosom. And he put his hand into his bosom: and when he took it out, his hand was leprous as snow.[7]And He said, Put your hand into thy bosom again. And he put his hand into his bosom again; and plucked it out of his bosom, and it was turned again as his other flesh".

Leprosy is a picture of sin. The disease of Leprosy was clearly examined in Leviticus and was a disease with prime importance among other diseases, where the sufferers where usually sent out of the camp of Israel. The priest payed special attention to the disease of Leprosy as does the Law. God used this particular miracle to tell Moses that they (Israelites and the world) were sinners and it's only God Himself that can cleanse sins.

Moses showed these two miracles to the Elders of Israel but showed only one; which is the rod turning into a snake to Pharoah (a symbol of Satan) but the one concerning his hand turning Leprous wasn't shown to Pharoah. So God was concealing the washing of sins which will be done by the greater Moses which is Jesus hidden from the knowledge of Satan.

The Rod of Moses – Shadow of the Cross

After Moses had met with God in a burning bush, the Rod of Moses became the Rod of God.

Exodus 4:20 "And Moses took his wife and his sons and set them on donkeys, and he returned to the land of Egypt; and Moses took the ROD OF GOD in his hands."

The Rod of God was used to do many miracles in the land of Egypt. After the Israelites went out of Egypt they camped by the Red sea beside Pihahiroth, in front of Baal-Zephon.

Pharaoh and his officials changed their minds and decided to pursue after Israel to bring them back to bondage: As Pharaoh approached, the Israelites looked up and saw the Egyptians coming after them. The Israelites were terrified and cried out to the Lord for help. Moses cried out to God.

Exodus 14:15-16 – "The Lord said to Moses, why do you cry to Me? Tell the people of Israel to go forward. Lift up your Rod and stretch out your hand over the sea and divide it, and the Israelites shall go on dry ground through the midst (middle) of the sea."

God asked Moses "Why do cry to Me? Might sound weird, because it was obvious that the Israelites needed God urgently in that situation. But what God wanted to point out to Moses, is that Moses already has the ROD OF GOD in his hands; symbolizing God's power. Let me use a clear example. If you have a loaded machine gun with you and you are surrounded with many terrorists with knives, do you go and start crying to the police for help? No, you open fire.

God has given us everything we need through the cross (the death of Jesus Christ) yet many Christians are still begging God to do what He has already done on the cross and heaven will be perplexed because of you.

At another instance, the whole congregation of Israel came into the desert of Zin in the First month and they stayed in Kadesh. There was no water for the Israelites and as usual, they murmured against God and Moses.

Exodus 17:4 "So Moses cried to the Lord, what shall I do with these people? They are almost ready to stone me and the Lord said to Moses, pass on before the people, and take with you some of the elders of Israel; and take in your hand the Rod with which you smote

the river (Nile), and go behold I God will stand before you "in front of" you there on the rock (mount) of Horeb; and you shall strike the rock, and water shall come out of it, that the people may drink, and Moses did so in the sight of the elders of Israel."

This Rod of God is a symbol of the cross and the Rock is a symbol of Jesus Christ.

1 Corinthians 10:4 "and they (Israel) all drank from a Spiritual Rock which followed them (produced by the sole power of God Himself without natural instrumentality), and the Rock was Christ."

When Moses struck the Rock, with the Rod (symbol of the cross) He struck Jesus Christ (symbolic for the striking on the Cross)

Numbers 20:10-11 "And Moses and Aaron gathered the assembly before the Rock. And he said to them, listen now, you rebels; shall we bring forth water for you out of this Rock? Then Moses lifted up his hands and struck the Rock Twice with his Rod; and water came forth abundantly, and the congregation and their beasts drank."

God instructed Moses to strike the Rock with the Rod once, Moses struck it twice and God was angry, because Jesus was to be struck with the cross (in death) once but since Moses struck the Rock twice, Moses will die the latter death before he could enter the promised land.

Numbers 20:12[12]And the LORD spake unto Moses and Aaron, Because ye believed me not, to sanctify me in the eyes of the children of Israel, therefore ye shall not bring this congregation into the land which I have given them.

The Passover Lamb

The deliverance of the Israelites from slavery in Egypt was the most remarkable miracle done in the old testament and the most revered and referenced by God. In so much that He instructed them to tell their generations to come. God brings this deliverance message to Israel when He wants to instruct, correct, bless them or when He wants to make a promise. It is all round the most revered both by God and Israel.

However this deliverance happened because of the Passover which in turn is the most revered and transcended to us as the "Holy Communion". So both the Passover and the Exodus are not mutually exclusive they actually go hand in hand.

Exodus 12:13[13]And the blood shall be to you for a token upon the houses where ye are: and when I see the blood, I will pass over you, and the plague shall not be upon you to destroy you, when I smite the land of Egypt.

The blood of the Passover lamb placed on their houses was just a toke(a symbol) as God said and the real

Passover lamb for the whole world will be Jesus; His Son. The blood of the Passover lamb was to be placed on their lintel and the lamb eaten with bitter herbs.

The whole story of the Passover and the Exodus from Egypt is just a picture showing us what the actual and greater Passover Lamb; Jesus would do on the Cross to redeem men from bondage and slavery to Satan. And we will be taking you on a more detailed Journey as to how Jesus fulfilled this highly revered Ceremony on the Cross.

1 Corinthians 5:7[7]Purge out therefore the old leaven, that ye may be a new lump, as ye are unleavened. For even Christ our Passover (Lamb) is sacrificed for us:

This shows the Passover Lamb in Egypt was a shadow and reality of the Passover Lamb is Christ Jesus.

The Israelites were held captives and made slaves for hundreds of years in Egypt and were sold into hard-labour. God raised up Moses for the purpose of delivering Israel from Egypt. After numerous warnings given to Pharoah coupled with a lot of signs and the ten plagues, Pharoah will not heed to the warnings.

Those plagues placed on Egypt was in effect telling them that He was greater than all the gods of Egypt with. From the plague of frogs to the plague of thick darkness. The Egyptians had gods they believed to control frogs, locusts, flies and the Sun. God bringing those plagues to them;

with the last plague of thick darkness directed to their Sun god (Ra). In effect, these plagues tells of His greatness over those gods. Other plagues followed too for other surrounding nations to know that the God of Israel was the only true God and hence abandon their own false gods: it was like a gospel then which only few like Rahab heeded are recorded.

Despite all the miracles and plagues shown to Pharoah, he still wouldn't budge but things were drastically about to change upon the institution of the Passover.

Exodus 12:1-4[1]And the LORD spake unto Moses and Aaron in the land of Egypt, saying,[2]This month shall be unto you the beginning of months: it shall be the first month of the year to you.[3]Speak ye unto all the congregation of Israel, saying, In the tenth day of this month they shall take to them every man a lamb, according to the house of their fathers, a lamb for an house:[4]And if the household be too little for the lamb, let him and his neighbour next unto his house take it according to the number of the souls; every man according to his eating shall make your count for the lamb.

The celebration of the Passover was to begin a new month and a new year for the Israelites. Just like anyone that comes to Christ has a clean slate in the eyes of God, they are a new creatures and in God's eyes they just actually started living.

In the fourth chapter of Genesis, it is the sacrifice of the lamb for each person. In the Passover it was a lamb for each house (Family). Upon the giving of the Law, it would be a lamb for the entire nation. But when Jesus came, He would be the lamb sacrificed for the entirety of the world.

John 1:29[29]The next day John seeth Jesus coming unto him, and saith, Behold the Lamb of God, which taketh away the sin of the world.

Jesus came to be the Passover lamb for the whole world, freeing us from God's eternal judgement of Sin and the oppression from Satan

Exodus 12:5[5]Your lamb shall be without blemish, a male of the first year: ye shall take it out from the sheep, or from the goats:

The lamb used for sacrifice was to be without blemish (or defect), must be a lamb of one year (young and in its prime).

Jesus was the only human without blemish (Sin). He didn't inherit the Sin of Adam, hence the necessity of the virgin birth. He wasn't conceived of a human seed. Jesus also died young (33 years) and in the prime of His Life. Jesus had to be sinless to be able to die for Sin. If He had sin, He too will be under the power of Satan. A prisoner cannot set another prisoner free.

2 Corinthians 5:21 "For He (God) hath made Him (Jesus) who knew no sin; that we might be made the righteousness of God in Him (Jesus).

The Sin of the whole world was placed on Jesus who is our substitute shielding us from God's judgement (like the ark of Noah).

The Passover celebration coincided with the Judgement of God upon the First born of Egypt

Exodus 12:11-13[11]And thus shall ye eat it; with your loins girded, your shoes on your feet, and your staff in your hand; and ye shall eat it in haste: it is the LORD'S Passover.[12]For I will pass through the land of Egypt this night, and will smite all the firstborn in the land of Egypt, both man and beast; and against all the gods of Egypt I will execute judgment: I am the LORD.[13]And the blood shall be to you for a token upon the houses where ye are: and when I see the blood, I will pass over you, and the plague shall not be upon you to destroy you, when I smite the land of Egypt.

The same Passover that shielded the Israelites from God's judgement, sealed the fate of the Egyptians, what was a solution for Israel was a huge problem for Egypt. Just as it is now, the Same Cross that was used to pay for the sins of the entire world will also seal the Judgement of God upon those who reject Jesus. The Same Cross that brought deliverance to mankind has sealed the Judgement upon Satan and his Kingdom.

In Egyptian mythology at that time, the Firstborn was the continuation of Life for the parent; they believed that their after-life was through their First-born. Not only were they crying because they lost their Children but even more horrible was that there was no after-life for them. It was like hell. The judgement upon the firstborn went down even to their animals and went up even to Pharoah's household. Pharoah was actually seen as a god in Egyptian culture so he too had to be personally judged as God judged all the gods of Egypt through the Passover. If it is to be noticed, they were to take the Passover in haste as God instructed. The only time we hear Jesus telling someone to make haste was in receiving Him: as He told Zaccheaus.

Luke 19:5[5]And when Jesus came to the place, he looked up, and saw him, and said unto him, Zacchaeus, make haste, and come down; for today I must abide at thy house.

God is telling the world to make haste to accept Jesus into their lives to avoid eternal judgement in hell.

Another thing to be noticed is that it was just the blood of the Passover on their houses that was the distinguishing mark, it was not about their actions if they were good or bad, or if they were rich or poor, some might have even been worshipping the gods of Egypt before and they didn't even have to be Israelites (there was a mixed multitude in the Exodus). It was only the blood of the Passover that shielded them from God's judgement. As it is now it doesn't matter if you are good or bad, if you have your life together or not it is accepting Jesus that matters and everything else in your actions will be addressed as you grow more in Christ.

Numbers 9:11-12[11]The fourteenth day of the second month at evening they shall keep it, and eat it with unleavened bread and bitter herbs.[12]They shall leave none of it unto the morning, nor break any bone of it: according to all the ordinances of the passover they shall keep it.

The Passover was to be a continuous ritual, to commemorate their deliverance from Egypt by God. The Passover lamb was to be brought on the tenth day and monitored to the fourteenth day when it would be killed, it should be eaten with unleavened bread (bread without yeast), with bitter herbs, it must be roasted with fire(not eaten raw) and none of its bone should be broken. Jesus fulfilled these aspects too.

From the time He officially went into the temple (the triumphant entry) where huge crowds welcomed and praised Him, the pharisees, sadducees, scribes and some jews monitored and tested Him with more intensity; looking for what to use against Him. History proves that Jesus died on the Fourteenth day of the month of Aviv. The unleavened bread speaks of the purity of Jesus as yeast signified impurity hence sin in this context.

1 Corinthians 5:7[7]Purge out therefore the old leaven, that ye may be a new lump, as ye are unleavened. For even Christ our passover is sacrificed for us:

Mark 8:15[15]And he charged them, saying, Take heed, beware of the leaven of the Pharisees, and of the leaven of Herod.

The bitter herbs speaks of the sufferings of Jesus as a man. Isaiah called Him a man of Sorrow (Isaiah 53). Jesus (the sin bearer of the world) came under the Fire of God's judgement, judging even the minute details Sin both externally and internally and finally even with all those immense torture no man has ever faced, even with the piercings both hands and legs, none of His Bones were broken. Wow.

The romans who invented the crucifixion were unconsciously fulfilling Bible Prophecy. They didn't know the passover Laws yet they helped in it's fulfillment.

John 19:31-36[31]The Jews therefore, because it was

the preparation, that the bodies should not remain upon the cross on the sabbath day, (for that sabbath day was an high day,) besought Pilate that their legs might be broken, and that they might be taken away.[32]Then came the soldiers, and brake the legs of the first, and of the other which was crucified with him.[33]But when they came to Jesus, and saw that he was dead already, they brake not his legs:[34]But one of the soldiers with a spear pierced his side, and forthwith came there out blood and water.[35]And he that saw it bare record, and his record is true: and he knoweth that he saith true, that ye might believe.[36]For these things were done, that the scripture should be fulfilled, A bone of him shall not be broken.

5 THE BRONZE SERPENT

The Lord God fought for the Israelites and gave them victory over Arad, the Canaanite king who attacked them and captured some of them. The Israelites cried to God, and God helped them. Then they continued their journey to Edom.

Numbers 21:4-6 "Then they set out from mount Hor by way of the Red sea to bypass the land of Edom, but the people became impatient because of the journey. The people spoke against God and Moses: "why have you led us up from Egypt to die in the wilderness? There is no bread or water and we detest this wretched food.. (referring to the manna) then the Lord sent poisonous snake among the people, and they bit them so that many Israelites died".

The Israelites spoke against God and Moses, God was angry at the Israelites he sent poisonous snakes that killed many of them.

Number 21:7-9 "and the people came to Moses, and said we have sinned, for we have spoken against the Lord and against you; pray to the Lord, that He may take away the serpents from us. So Moses pray to the Lord, that He may take away the serpents from us. So Moses prayed for the people. And the Lord said to Moses, make a fiery serpent (a snake image) of bronze and set it on a pole; and everyone who is bitten, when he looks at it, shall live. And Moses made a serpent of bronze and put it on a pole (wood), and if a serpent had

bitten any man, when he looked to the serpent of bronze (attentively, expectantly, with a steady and absorbing gage), he lived".

After the snakes had bitten the people and the people cried to God". Moses with God's instruction made a bronze (brass) snake image and hung it on a pole in a mountain. That bronze snake is symbolic of Jesus. The bronze snake looked like the snakes that bit the Israelites but did not have the poison. Just like Jesus made to look like man but did not have the sin nature. The bronze serpent was put on a pole (wood) on a mountain just like Jesus was placed on a pole (wooden cross) on a mountain (mount Calvary to be exact).

John 3:14-15 "Jesus said and just as Moses lifted up the serpent (bronze serpent) in the desert (on a pole), so must the Son of Man (Jesus referring to Himself) be lifted up (on the cross)".

The Bible said that any that looked (beheld) the bronze snake would be healed. However there may have some who did not look at the bronze snake on the pole and the mountain they were busy looking at their problems and did not receive healing hence died.

That's the same way it is today; when you behold Jesus in the bible you will receive your healing. The devil may try to discourage you but keep on seeing Jesus in His word ask the Holy- Spirit to help you.

In Judaism Bronze (Brass) signifies judgement, that was what the outer part of the altar used in the temple to sacrifice animals was made of. That bronze serpent was symbolic for Jesus taking God's righteous judgement upon Himself.

He died for the sins of the world. However only those who believe in Jesus will receive that. It's one thing for something to be paid for and another thing for someone to receive what has been paid for.

It is still possible for many people go to hell even though their sins have been paid for just because they did not believe in Jesus Christ.

6 DAVID AND MEPHIBOSHET

2 Samuel 4:4 "Jonathan, Saul's son, had a son who was a cripple in his feet. He was five years old when the news came out of Jezreel (of the death) of Saul and Jonathan. And the boy's nurse took him up and fled, and in her haste, he fell and became lame. His name was Mephibosheth."

2 Samuel 9:1-7 "David asked, is there anyone remaining from Saul's family I can show kindness to because of JONATHAN? There was a servant of Saul's family name Ziba. They summoned him to David, and the king said to him, "Are you Ziba?" I am your servant, he replied. So the king asked is there anyone left of Saul's family I can show the kindness of God to? Ziba said to king David, "there is still Jonathan's son who is lame in both feet." The king asked him, where is he? Ziba answered the king, you will find him in Lo-debar at the house of Machir son of Ammiel in Lodebar. Mephibosheth son of Jonathan son of Saul came to David, bowed down to the ground and paid homage. David said, "Mephibosheth" I am your servant, "he replied don't be afraid, David said to him, "since I intend to show you kindness because of your father Jonathan. I will restore to you all your grandfather Saul's fields, and you will eat at my table."

Mephibosheth bowed down and said, what is your servant that you take an interest in a dead dog like me?"

David wanted to show the kindness of God to anyone remaining in Saul's family because of who was lame was brought to him and David planned to show abundant kindness on him.

Mephibosheth replied "what is your servant that you take interest in a dead dog like me". Mephibosheth was very scared of David, thinking David was bent on destroying every descendant of Saul and take over everything.

Saul was envious, obsessed and paranoid concerning David. He wouldn't miss an opportunity to speak evil against him.

From the time David killed Goliath when he was younger, and when the women sang "Saul killed a thousand, David killed ten thousand" Saul became jealous and tried everything in his power to kill David.

David had many opportunities to kill Saul but did not. In contrast Jonathan; Saul's Son loved David like a brother and saved David from the hands of his Father.

Saul must have made David look like a despicable man in the eyes of Mephibosheth; that's why he was so afraid of David, but when he was brought to David, he saw a very different situation. David showed so much kindness to Mephibosheth it shocked Mephibosheth to the core. He did it because of Jonathan.

2 Samuel 9:9-13 "Then the king summoned Saul's attendant (servant) Ziba and said to him, I have given

your master's grandson all that belonged to Saul and his family. You, your sons, and your servants are to work the ground for him, and you are to bring in (the crops) so your master's (Saul's) grandson, is always to eat at my table. "Now Ziba had 15 sons and 20 servants." Ziba said to the king, "your servants will do all my lord the king commands. So Mephibosheth ate at David's table just like one of the kings sons. Mephibosheth had a young son whose name was Mica. All those living in Ziba's house were Mephibosheth's servants. However, Mephibosheth lived in Jerusalem because he always ate at the kings table. He was lame in both feet."

David continued to show the kindness of God to Mephibosheth, David made his servants to be Mephibosheth's servants, Mephibosheth was like an Adopted son, he ate at the kings table like one of the king's son and stayed in Jerusalem, with him.

David in this context symbolized God the Father, Jonathan symbolized Jesus, Mephibosheth is symbolic to us, we fell in the garden of Eden and became disfigured as Mephibosheth fell when he was a baby. Like Mephibosheth, many of us have been thought by religion of a God who is wicked, angry, a strict disciplinary and a God who is looking for excuses to punish us.

So much good was done to Mephibosheth because of Jonathan, just as God has blessed us with every spiritual blessings in Christ and shown us much love, acceptance and grace because of Him.

Mephibosheth expected David to be wicked, to destroy him and take what he had but when Mephibosheth was brought to David, he saw something entirely different. The same thing when we came to God, God envelopes us with His unconditional love and grace, the ultimate love God showed to mankind is sending His own Son Jesus to die in our place on the cross of Calvary. King David treated Mephibosheth like his adopted son.

Because of Jesus death on the cross we too have been adopted as sons (or daughters) of God.

Galatians 4:4-7[4]But when the fulness of the time was come, God sent forth his Son, made of a woman, made under the law,[5]To redeem them that were under the law, that we might receive the adoption of sons.[6]And because ye are sons, God hath sent forth the Spirit of his Son into your hearts, crying, Abba, Father.[7]Wherefore thou art no more a servant, but a son; and if a son, then an heir of God through Christ.

7 THE TWO WATERS

I was studying the book of Exodus God began to show me things. He gave me an analogy of the total redemption of Israel and the Church

The Total redemption of Israel (in context of leaving Egypt and going into the land) in was brought about by the Crossing of two waters which are the red sea and river Jordan.

Two waters but one method of redemption (the same way they walked on dry land in between the walls of water). Telling us that the Cross is both for Redemption and Sanctification (it's for the sinner and the Saint). Moses was the progenitor of the first, Joshua of the Second. Moses in this first case was a picture of God (as was insinuated by God in the burning bush) as the Source of the Cross, Joshua a picture of the Spirit was the continuer and Israel being the picture of the Church.

God the Father is the source of salvation while the Spirit is in charge of sanctification. Redemption from Egypt signified leaving bondage of Sin and all Satan's forces while the crossing of the Jordan was to drive out the perizites, hivites and attack d inhabitants of Jericho(which was picture of the flesh we are to attack).

In the first instance it was the Egyptians that were going

to attack Israel which God foiled but now it's Israel going to attack Jericho. So the first instance of Egypt it was all God's workings but in the second instance of Jordan the Israelites had a role to play (which is symbolism for God being the Sole source responsible for our Redemption but we have a role to play in Sanctification).

In the first instance they had No steady presence of God in context of the ark, but while Crossing the Jordan they had the Ark. Telling us that though God lives in Us, we still need to renew our minds by the message of Christ.

In the first instance of Egypt, God told them to STANDSTILL but at the river Jordan He told them to step their feet into the water (symbolic for walking with or in the Spirit) which they obeyed and got eventually into the Promised Land. Just like when we walk in the Spirit, hear and obey we will get into God's intention for the Believer (which is to be like Christ)

8 THE SPECIAL LESSON OF JOB

The issue with Job is that he had a lot of confidence in his sacrifices and goodness. But like we are made to understand that no amount of goodness can save man from the Sin nature apart from Jesus. Job though good that even God highly commended, still possessed it and Satan could still legally ask for him.

What God was trying to make him and us understand is that we all carry the Sin nature and no amount of good can change it.

Job so relied on the goodness of Self and by this example God shows us that even Self in terms of good works cannot save you but Jesus Christ. This is a direct warning to those who reject Christ but think their good works will suffice. Forgetting that even the tree of knowledge of good and evil also had good in it and God wants us to eat of the tree of Life which is now Christ. Job in his despair and anguish sook for a mediator between Him and God and a Redeemer.

Though with vague understanding, he needed who will bring him to God or plead his case. A prayer that would be answered centuries later by Jesus coming down to die for man hence becoming the bridge between God and Man

Job 9:1-2[1]Then Job answered and said,[2]I know it is so of a truth: but how should man be just(righteous) with God?

This is a question that could only be answered in Jesus, because it is only in Christ we can be declared righteous before God. And man on his own irrespective of his goodness cannot be righteous before God.

Job 9:3-4[3]If he will contend with Him, he cannot answer him one of a thousand.[4]He is wise in heart, and mighty in strength: who hath hardened himself against Him, and hath prospered?

Nobody can stand before God and respond to His questions. Job learned this the hard way when he was finally given his audience.

At the end of the chapter, Job explained the problem and necessary solution:

Job 9:32-33[32]For he is not a man, as I am, that I should answer him, and we should come together in judgment.[33]Neither is there any days-man(mediator) between us, that might lay his hand upon us both.

Job longed for a Mediator to stand between God and him. What Job longed for is now our reality.

1 Timothy 2:5[5]For there is one God, and one mediator

between God and men, the man Christ Jesus;

The words "lay his hand on us both" refer to bringing people together, which is how it is translated in some Bibles. Job was looking for a person to reconcile him to God, and 2 Corinthians 5:18 says, "God has reconciled us to Himself through Jesus Christ."

2 Corinthians 5:18-19[18]And all things are of God, who hath reconciled us to himself by Jesus Christ, and hath given to us the ministry of reconciliation;[19]To wit, that God was in Christ, reconciling the world unto himself, not imputing their trespasses unto them; and hath committed unto us the word of reconciliation.

Job 9:34-35[34]Let him take his rod away from me, and let not his fear terrify me:

A rod administers punishment, and Job wanted the Mediator to take away the judgment he deserved. But if God took it from him, He would have to administer the punishment to someone else. Sins can't go unpunished or God not be just. Job expected his Mediator to receive his punishment

Isaiah 53:5[5]But He(Jesus) was wounded for our transgressions, He was bruised for our iniquities: the chastisement of our peace was upon Him; and with His

stripes we are healed.

Job 9:35[35]Then would I speak, and not fear him; but it is not so with me.

Job could approach God confidently if the Mediator did what he described, but he knew that had not been done for him. Jesus has done this for us though: "We have boldness and access [to God] with confidence through faith in [Jesus]" (Ephesians 3:12).

Job with these words, seemed to be getting the whole reason of this trial but yet again he defaulted back into Self, back to his good works. Job gave his impeccable Resume' of good works and high moral standing, he was yet to understand that even the good part of self still belonged to that forbidden tree and both the good and evil caused man to be driven out.

Of course God commends us for good works, it is not where our confidence should rest on but on the finished work of Christ. Salvation can lead to good works, but good works cannot lead to salvation.

Job in his frustration, anger and confusion wanted an audience with God so that he could say his mind directly to Him. But alas after getting His audience from God, Job's reply changed

Job 40:4[4]Behold, I am vile; what shall I answer thee? I

will lay mine hand upon my mouth.

This is the point that God wanted to show Job: that every man is under the sin nature and that trusting in self; even in good self is not good enough. Every man inherited the sin nature primarily because of Adam's sin: the sin that passed to all men. It is only in Christ we are free from that Sin. Job needed to come to the end of himself. The same thing that Isaiah the Prophet.

Isaiah was sent to pronounce warnings and Judgement on people and Kings. Pronouncing several woes on them. But when he came to the Presence of God, he realized that he was also a sinner and exclaimed "Woe is me"

Isaiah 6:1-5[1]In the year that king Uzziah died I saw also the Lord sitting upon a throne, high and lifted up, and his train filled the temple.[2]Above it stood the Seraphims: each one had six wings; with twain he covered his face, and with twain he covered his feet, and with twain he did fly.[3]And one cried unto another, and said, Holy, holy, holy, is the LORD of hosts: the whole earth is full of his glory.[4]And the posts of the door moved at the voice of him that cried, and the house was filled with smoke.[5]Then said I, Woe is me! for I am undone; because I am a man of unclean lips, and I dwell in the midst of a people of unclean lips: for mine eyes have seen the King, the LORD of hosts.

When Isaiah saw the Lord, he realized that he too was vile. This is the realization God wants us to come to; to know that we all need a Saviour; we all need cleansing and that which can only be provided by Jesus and the Cross which the Altar symbolized. The Lord which Isaiah saw was actually the pre-incarnate appearance of Christ.

This was one of the primary reason why the Law of Moses was given: To bring all men to the end of themselves. To make Israel realize that this Law of over 600 commandments cannot be kept, hence the need for a savior and that was what the sacrifice represented. God gave that system of sacrifice as a loophole since He knew it is humanly not possible to keep all.

After Job started to realize what all this was all about, God took his attention to the Leviathan which was symbol of Satan based on the description given.

The book of Job was the first time Satan was introduced. It is the oldest book in the Bible written by Moses. It is estimated that Job lived at the time of Abraham.

God introduced Job to his actual enemy and His own enemy. He told job the CV of Satan; telling him that nothing can bring this enemy down except him. Satan is older, wiser and stronger than man. But God is older, wiser and infinitely stronger than Satan. And that only in Jesus Christ and the Cross that we are given power over

Sin and satan. The foundation of all Sin was Pride; Satan's very own invention which led to his downfall as Lucifer. Pride is also the foundational sin that caused the Fall of Adam and Eve in the garden. They wanted to do things without God and wanted to be like Him (which they already where). God resists the proud.

After God had finished talking to Job, Job then came to the full realization that indeed all men are sinners and need a saviour

Isaiah 64:6[6]But we are all as an unclean thing, and all our righteousnesses are as filthy rags; and we all do fade as a leaf; and our iniquities, like the wind, have taken us away.

It didn't say our sins are like filthy rags, It said our Righteousness. No amount of human Righteousness can reach God's standard: only the righteousness of His Son Jesus given freely to them that believe. This is what God wants everyone to understand and embrace. Job had finally gotten it.

Job 42:5-6[5]I have heard of thee by the hearing of the ear: but now mine eye seeth thee.[6]Wherefore I abhor myself, and repent in dust and ashes.

The same repentance God is calling for mankind. Repentance here is turning to Jesus; placing your faith in

His death on the Cross; He is our substitute.

9 THE LESSON OF GEHAZI

The punishment of Gehazi gives a dire warning to those who not only see the message of God as a business enterprise and those who preach another Jesus. But before we get to Gehazi, there are more important issues we should look at first.

Naaman was one of the most successful military captains in his day more so that the country he was from and fought for where like the rulers of the world at that time. But even at that, Naaman was a leper.

2 Kings 5:1[1]Now Naaman, captain of the host of the king of Syria, was a great man with his master, and honourable, because by him the LORD had given deliverance unto Syria: he was also a mighty man in valour, but he was a leper.

As we have learned how leprosy is a type of sinful nature. The Leviticus payed so much attention to this disease than anything else.

Naaman had all these titles, accomplishments and accolade yet he was still a leper that needed Healing, he couldn't help himself: This is the state of many in the world today: they are powerful, wealthy, gurus in their fields and have a lot of accolades and yet are still Spiritual lepers under sin.

Naaman(a gentile) sought for help for his leprosy to no avail but a Hebrew slave girl drew his attention to Elisha the Prophet; a man of God in Israel who could cure the Leprosy. Naaman set out to find Elisha bringing with him alot of treasures with him.

2 Kings 5:9-10[9]So Naaman came with his horses and with his chariot, and stood at the door of the house of Elisha.[10]And Elisha sent a messenger unto him, saying, Go and wash in Jordan seven times, and thy flesh shall come again to thee, and thou shalt be clean.

Naaman came to the house of Elisha expecting a grand welcome befitting for a king after all he was the right hand man to the greatest king of that time but unfortunately for him, none of that happened. He was also told to wash in the muddy waters of Jordan seven times

2 Kings 5:11[11]But Naaman was wroth, and went away, and said, Behold, I thought, He will surely come out to me, and stand, and call on the name of the LORD his God, and strike his hand over the place, and recover the leper.

Naaman's pride made him extremely angry, almost getting in the way of his healing. Elisha not only didn't come out to greet him but also told him to wash in the Jordan River seven times. How can a man in his position do that? Naaman also wanted some mystical demonstration of the Divine in curing his Leprosy.

Every individual whether great or small, rich or poor, beautiful or ugly, good or bad must come the same way to be cleansed of their spiritual leprosy which is Sin. Naaman thought he was too big to wash in the Jordan river to be cleansed of his disease.

2 Kings 5:12[12]Are not Abana and Pharpar, rivers of Damascus, better than all the waters of Israel? may I not wash in them, and be clean? So he turned and went away in a rage.

The rivers of Abana and Pharpar were the clearest streams in the world; and we the way Naaman put it, it must have been streams people of high status usually wash in. Naaman was angry that Elisha didn't choose these beautiful rivers but chose the ordinary Jordan river.

The Jordan river in this context symbolized the Cross. Just as it was the only river that could cleanse Naaman's leprosy, the Cross is the only way to cleanse our Sins. Remember Blood and water gushed out from the side of Jesus as He hung on the Cross.

As beautiful as those rivers where, they couldn't cleanse Naaman's disease. If you will notice in the old testament time the word "healed" is not used for leprosy but the word Cleansed is used.

2 Kings 5:13[13]And his servants came near, and spake unto him, and said, My father, if the prophet had bid thee do some great thing, wouldest thou not have done it? how much rather then, when he saith to thee, Wash, and be clean?

Men are ever looking for how to earn salvation. Some have done many rites, gone into false religions, some are depending on their good works when in reality all you have to do is to acknowledge Jesus death on the Cross to receive this salvation. Some can't fathom that believing in this old rugged cross could cleanse their sins.

But ultimately, Naaman dropped his pride and went down to wash in the River Jordan.

2 Kings 5:14[14]Then went he down, and dipped himself seven times in Jordan, according to the saying of the man of God: and his flesh came again like unto the flesh of a little child, and he was clean.

After Naaman had washed in the Jordan River, he was completely cleansed to such a high degree that it looked like that of a Child: he got a little extra. There's no magic in washing in the river seven times, only that it is a number that denoted God's total redemption. Jesus cried on the Cross "It is Finished". He secured a total cleansing for the world at least all those who believes in Him.

Naaman came to the acknowledgement that the God is the only true God of all the Earth. He brought alot of treasures to Elisha as a gift but Elisha refused to collect it.

2 Kings 5:15-16[15]And he returned to the man of God, he and all his company, and came, and stood before him: and he said, Behold, now I know that there is no God in all the earth, but in Israel: now therefore, I pray thee, take a blessing of thy servant.[16]But he said, As the LORD liveth, before whom I stand, I will receive none. And he urged him to take it; but he refused.

But Elisha did receive gifts at other times, why not this time?Because this whole episode was a picture portraying God's grace. Nobody can pay for God's grace. Money and good works cannot earn God's grace. If Elisha had taken money or gifts, it would have immediately cancelled out God's grace. It would have made a mockery of God's power and ultimately the power of the Cross.

Unfortunately there are many of these pastors or prophet that have turned the gospel into merchandise. It's now about buying and selling similar to those that Jesus drove out of the Temple. They have turned the grace of God into wages hence a warning was sent to them through the experience of Gehazi.

2 Kings 5:20[20]But Gehazi, the servant of Elisha the man of God, said, Behold, my master hath spared Naaman this Syrian, in not receiving at his hands that which he brought: but, as the LORD liveth, I will run after him, and take somewhat of him.

Gehazi initiates his efforts to change the great plan of salvation from "the Grace of God" to "Salvation by works" it was met, as we shall see with severe Judgement

2 Kings 5:21-22[21]So Gehazi followed after Naaman. And when Naaman saw him running after him, he lighted down from the chariot to meet him, and said, Is all well?[22]And he said, All is well. My master hath sent me, saying, Behold, even now there be come to me from mount Ephraim two young men of the sons of the prophets: give them, I pray thee, a talent of silver, and two changes of garments.

So Gehazi cooked up a story so as to get some gifts from Naaman lying with Elisha's name.

This is the same issue we have in the modern Church they have exchanged the Grace of God for money, many cook up stories lying with the name of Jesus to manipulate people for their money. Their goal is not to preach the message of Christ but to get money. Of course the Church needs money but substituting the message of the Cross, lying about receiving messages and visions from God in a bid to manipulate children of God, is a serious offence as we shall see.

2 Kings 5:25-26[25]But he went in, and stood before his master. And Elisha said unto him, Whence comest thou, Gehazi? And he said, Your servant went no whither.[26]And he said unto him, Went not mine heart with thee, when the man turned again from his chariot to meet you? Is it a time to receive money, and to receive garments, and olive yards, and vineyards, and sheep, and oxen, and menservants, and maidservants?

God had already revealed the whole Episode of Gehazi to Elisha; God was angry and Elisha was angry too. Elisha asked him if now is the time to start collecting gifts?

The same can be asked to so many preachers today. The world is dying without God, people are going to hell, are under the oppression of Satan and your focus and preaching is about money?

2 Kings 5:27[27]The leprosy therefore of Naaman shall cleave unto thee, and unto thy seed forever. And he went out from his presence a leper as white as snow.

Gehazi's attempt to change the Grace of God into works was met with severe Judgement. You'll wonder how Gehazi who was Elisha's servant for years would be cursed so severely by his master. However this whole episode was even bigger than Elisha. This is Gehazi trying to change the pattern of grace into that of works which God will not tolerate.

This is the same dire warning God is sending to those who substitute the message of the Cross for another thing hence preaching another Jesus. We don't know what punishment will be dished out to those who do such things but the New testament gives us a hint.

Galatians 1:8[8] But though we, or an angel from heaven, preach any other gospel unto you than that which we have preached unto you, let him be accursed.

Paul said even he, or even an Angel from heaven should preach another gospel hence another Jesus, such person is under a curse from God. Paul repeated it again for emphasis and urgency.

Galatians 1:9[9]As we said before, so say I now again, If any man preach any other gospel unto you than that ye have received, let him be accursed.

10 THE LESSON ON BALAAM

Balaam was a very peculiar kind of Prophet spoken about in the Bible. However he was actually put into a negative light especially in the New testament scriptures for some very interesting yet solid reason.

Balaam came into the picture when Balak; the king of the Moabites was so afraid of Israel, because he and the surrounding nations heard what God did to the Egyptians that had enslaved them: How God had used so many miracles, plagues and the dreadful opening of the red sea to punish the Egyptians and how the surrounding nations that attacked Israel were decimated.

Numbers 22:1-3[1]And the children of Israel set forward, and pitched in the plains of Moab on this side Jordan by Jericho.[2]And Balak the son of Zippor saw all that Israel had done to the Amorites.[3]And Moab was sore afraid of the people, because they were many: and Moab was distressed because of the children of Israel.

Even though these same Israelites were just passing through his Land; Balak became extremely paranoid and hired a prophet with a reputation to place a curse on the Israelites so that they would be utterly destroyed.

Numbers 22:5-6[5]He sent messengers therefore unto Balaam the son of Beor to Pethor, which is by the river

of the land of the children of his people, to call him, saying, Behold, there is a people come out from Egypt: behold, they cover the face of the earth, and they abide over against me:[6]Come now therefore, I pray thee, curse me this people; for they are too mighty for me: peradventure I shall prevail, that we may smite them, and that I may drive them out of the land: for I wot that he whom thou blessest is blessed, and he whom thou cursest is cursed.

Balaam was evidently visited by the Nobles sent by King Balak to relay the instruction to curse the Israelites. Balaam had a reputation of cursing or blessing people and they will actually be cursed or blessed as the case may be. He received the instructions and made his plans to carry them out.

Numbers 22:8[8]And he said unto them, Lodge here this night, and I will bring you word again, as the LORD shall speak unto me: and the princes of Moab abode with Balaam.

It's surprising that Balaam who knew God didn't know about the Israelites and he was asking God if he should curse God's own people, the very people's He redeemed from Egypt and who He helped destroy the surrounding nations. It seems Balaam was a prophet not actually close to God. The source of his mystical powers to curse and to bless them comes into question.

Numbers 22:9[9]And God came unto Balaam, and said, What men are these with thee?

God knew who they were but still asked. The same way He asked Adam "Who told you you were naked?"

Numbers 22:10-12[10]And Balaam said unto God, Balak the son of Zippor, king of Moab, hath sent unto me, saying,[11]Behold, there is a people come out of Egypt, which covereth the face of the earth: come now, curse me them; peradventure I shall be able to overcome them, and drive them out.[12]And God said unto Balaam, Thou shalt not go with them; thou shalt not curse the people: for they are blessed.

God forbade Balaam from going with the nobles king Balak sent, telling him that he couldn't curse his people. Balaam related this message to them who evidently told King Balak. However Balak made a bigger offer, sending even more honourable nobles and promising honour and promotion for Balaam. Balaam however made a sham rejection of the offer even though as we would evidently see, his heart was in the gifts.

Numbers 22:19-20[19]Now therefore, I pray you, tarry ye also here this night, that I may know what the LORD will say unto me more.[20]And God came unto Balaam at night, and said unto him, If the men come to call thee, rise up, and go with them; but yet the word which I shall

say unto thee, that shalt thou do.

God had already instructed Balaam not to go with the nobles before, why is he still asking God about it? Because he didn't actually want to obey, he wanted the treasures of Balak. Since he would have disobeyed and still gone, God permitted him.

Balaam was well on his way to meet Balak and to curse Israel. On his way, something phenomenal happened. God opened the eyes of the horse Balaam was riding on to see the Angel sent against him. It tried to avoid the Angel but finally fell down when the Angel stood directly in front of it. Balaam oblivious to the happenings hit the horse(ass) with his staff in anger.

Numbers 22:28-29[28]And the LORD opened the mouth of the ass, and she said unto Balaam, What have I done unto thee, that thou hast smitten me these three times?[29]And Balaam said unto the ass, Because thou hast mocked me: I would there were a sword in mine hand, for now would I kill thee.

Balaam was so fixated on his greed that a talking horse didn't seem to faze him. This reveals the stubborn state of man's heart, showing that even signs and wonders cannot convert a heart that has decided to be unconverted.

Many times in old testament, God showed wonders to men and to nations yet they refused to believe in Him. Some examples are when God punished cities in Philistines for stealing the ark, they witnessed wonders yet instead of converting to God, they returned the ark and continued worshipping their fallen god "Dagon". These repeated itself in Egypt, among the Amorite kings and many more people. Only very few like Rahab was converted by the wonders of God. Signs and wonders couldn't convert the world then, hence the need for the Holy Spirit to help us believe. The Holy Spirit is of big benefit even to the unsaved world.

Three times God used the horse to give a lesson to Balaam: God also used this horse as a means for Balaam to judge himself. Balaam wanted to kill the horse that had served him for years because of he perceived disobedience. The same judgement that should have been meted out on him.

Numbers 22:31-33[31]Then the LORD opened the eyes of Balaam, and he saw the angel of the LORD standing in the way, and his sword drawn in his hand: and he bowed down his head, and fell flat on his face.[32]And the angel of the LORD said unto him, Wherefore hast thou smitten thine ass these three times? behold, I went out to withstand thee, because thy way is perverse before me:[33]And the ass saw me, and turned from me these

three times: unless she had turned from me, surely now also I had slain thee, and saved her alive.

The Lord opened the eyes of Balaam to see the Angel with a drawn sword and he fell faced down. The Angel emphasized on the "three times" the horse tried to avoid Him and that he would have been a dead man if not for the horse he had beaten because of disobedience.

Numbers 22:35[35]And the angel of the LORD said unto Balaam, Go with the men: but only the word that I shall speak unto thee, that thou shalt speak. So Balaam went with the princes of Balak.

There's something about the way this particular Angel spoke; as if He was God Himself with the phrases "because your way is perverse before me" and the same instruction God gave "but only the word I speak to you you shall speak". Well He is: This is actually the pre-incarnate appearance of Jesus.

However Balaam's heart didn't seem to have changed despite this whole experience. He was still back to his old tricks.

Numbers 23:1[1]And Balaam said unto Balak, Build me here seven altars, and prepare me here seven oxen and seven rams.

There's actually no mention of Seven altars in the

sacrificial system, there's only one altar. Balaam instituted his own revised form; maybe he thought it could impress God or something, by default Balaam was sacrificing to another god.

Balaam is not just disobeying, he is also profaning the sacrificial system. The same way that many churches and their leaders have left the sacrificial system (the Cross of Jesus) to preach or focus on other things like motivation, prosperity and the likes and by default, they are worshipping another Jesus or preaching another gospel.

Numbers 23:4-5[4]And God met Balaam: and he said unto him, I have prepared seven altars, and I have offered upon every altar a bullock and a ram.[5]And the LORD put a word in Balaam's mouth, and said, Return unto Balak, and thus thou shalt speak.

Balaam then began to speak to God about his preparing of his seven altars and sacrificing on them in a bid to impress God even on his disobedience or convince God to change His mind and allow him curse Israel. But as we see, God brushed that aside like He didn't hear what he said. The same way God doesn't pay attention to any doctrine or focus that is not about the Cross of Christ.

Why God keep talking with Balaam in spite of his numerous errors and a greedy heart we don't know. Bal upaam was even more diabolical; reasons we will see later as we proceed. However God still instructed Balaam on what to say.

God gave him a prophecy about Israel that had blessings attached to it. Balak brought Balaam to another part of their camp with the notion that Balaam's curse will still prevail. Balaam followed the same process as the first and God gave him another prophecy attached with blessings. The third time the same process was repeated but there's something interesting that was revealed at the time of the third prophecy.

Numbers 24:1[1]And when Balaam saw that it pleased the LORD to bless Israel, he went not, as at other times, to seek for enchantments, but he set his face toward the wilderness.

Evidently Balaam wasn't happy that God insisted on blessing Israel, this time he turned his face to the wilderness instead of facing Israel's camp as he previously did on top of mount Pisgah. The more surprising thing is the phrase "he went not as other times to seek for enchantments" trying to tell is that this same Balaam was also consulting witchcraft. So he spoke to God and also to demons. With this we can see that there are some who claim to be doing the work of God yet get their powers, inspiration and drive from demonic spirits(probably God in the morning, demons at night). This was a great deal of Blasphemy from the side of Balaam. However God was still using him and he blessed Israel the third time.

Balaam made a fourth prophecy concerning Israel. This prophecy was very peculiar because it pointed not only to Israel but to a particular figure.

Numbers 24:17[17]I shall see him, but not now: I shall behold him, but not nigh: there shall come a Star out of Jacob, and a Sceptre shall rise out of Israel, and shall smite the corners of Moab, and destroy all the children of Sheth.

This verse speaks of Jesus; pointing out that He was to come but not at that point in time: "there shall come a star out of Jacob" speaking of Jesus Christ, He is the prominent head of Israel for all times.

There's also a possibility that it was this prophecy about a Star that inspired the three wise men who were astrologers to not only believe it but to use it to locate Jesus at his birth. This is one of the Foundation for Joseph Seiss's book " The Gospel in the stars".

"A scepter shall rise out of Israel" speaking of the Authority, Kingship and dominion of Christ that would be fully expressed in His second coming.

Since Balaam had seen that God did not curse Israel he conspired to make Israel bring a curse on themselves. He set the Israelites up with the daughters of Moab who turned their heart from God to idols hence the bringing of deadly plagues that killed thousands.

Numbers 31:16[16]Behold, these caused the children of Israel, through the counsel of Balaam, to commit trespass against the LORD in the matter of Peor, and there was a plague among the congregation of the LORD.

Balaam's conspiracy actually worked. Those enchantments may have given him this idea.

We have gotten the reason why the Bible casts a negative light against Balaam. He not only disobeyed God but cast a stumbling block against Israel. Peter shed more light on Balaam and People especially Leaders like him.

2Peter2.14-16[14]They commit adultery with their eyes, and their lust is never satisfied. They make a game of luring unstable people into sin. They train themselves to be greedy; they are doomed and cursed.[15]They have wandered off the right road and followed the way of Balaam son of Beor, who loved to earn money by doing wrong.[16] But Balaam was stopped from his mad course when his donkey rebuked him with a human voice.

Such people use the work of God as a business scheme. They follow their own lust. They pervert the Bible in order to deceive people. They have made up their minds to be greedy and follow their own lusts that they reject warnings and profane the name of God. They are wolves in Sheep's clothing which bring hurt to believers in Christ and weakening their faith in Him because of their actions.

2Peter 2.17-18 These people are as useless as dried-up springs of water or as clouds blown away by the wind--promising much and delivering nothing. They are doomed to blackest darkness.[18]They brag about themselves with empty, foolish boasting, vain words. With lustful desire as their bait, they lure back into sin those who have just escaped from such wicked living.

These people are like tombs with a nice exterior but filled with dead men's bones. They like to boast about themselves, claim to be oracles of Christ and take people back to the sins they had left. These people are great orators like Balaam but act under a different spirit that is not of God.

With the way Balaam said the prophecies, it gives us a hint he was an orator, a master of words, he had flare: a lights, camera, action kind of prophet. Such people possess enticing words of man's wisdom.

2Peter 2.19[19]They promise freedom, but they themselves are slaves to sin and corruption. For you are a slave to whatever controls you.[20] And when people

escape from the wicked ways of the world by learning about our Lord and Savior Jesus Christ and then get tangled up with sin and become its slave again, they are worse off than before.

The condemnation of Balaam's actions and those like him didn't stop there.

Jude.1.11 How terrible it will be for them! For they follow the evil example of Cain, who killed his brother. Like Balaam, they will do anything for money. And like Korah, they will perish because of their rebellion.

Revelation 2.14 And yet I have a few complaints against you. You tolerate some among you who are like Balaam, who showed Balak how to trip up the people of Israel. He taught them to worship idols by eating food offered to idols and by committing sexual sin.

11 LAW AND GRACE

As with the cases of Job and Isaiah spoken about in the previous chapter, the Law of Moses was given for the same reason of bringing Man to the end of himself and showing him he was a sinner hence the need for a saviour.

A problem we can see with the Law is that though it was good, it only showed man as a sinner but had no power whatsoever to change Man. It's just like a mirror, it shows you your true self but has no power whatsoever to fix anything wrong

Galatians 3:19 "What then was the purpose of the Law? It was added (later on after the promise to disclose and expose men to guilt (sin) because of transgressions and (to make men more conscious of their sinfulness) of sin: and it was intended to be in effect until the Seed (Jesus Christ, the descendant, the Heir) should come, to and concerning whom the promise had been made. And it (the Law) was arranged and ordained and appointed through the instrumentality of angels (and was given) by the hand (in person) of a go-between. [Moses, an intermediary person between God and man].

The Law was given to call men to their sins until Jesus would come.

Romans 3:20 "Therefore, no one will be declared

righteous (Justified) in His (God's) sight by observing the LAW; rather through the Law we become conscious of sin."

The Commandments says "you shall not commit adultery" but did not say "Love your wives" it says you shall not steal, but did not say "Give", it says you shall not bear false witness against your neighbor but did not say love your neighbor, the Law says "you shall not covet "but did not say be content". Grace teaches us that and Jesus came to help us do that.

The Law was good while it lasted but it could not transform lives for the better, it was just there to make people conscious of their sins, show people that they need a Saviour, and appreciate the promised grace which we have now.

However some people keep the Law (in context of the Ten Commandments) for the wrong reasons, they might not steal because there is no real opportunity, they might not commit adultery because they are being monitored or not had the opportunity. Some obey the Ten Commandments not because they honour God but because they are afraid of punished. When you come to embrace God's grace you will start doing good works (actions) for the right reasons, you will honour and obey God for the right reasons.

The Law is made up of 600 ordinances and Ten Commandments. During the Law, any discharge makes you unclean until evening: probably with tears, saliva etc.

The woman that had the issue of blood and got healed after touching the hem of Jesus garment was actually breaking the Law of Moses by staying around people; because her bodily discharge made her unclean. If she was found out by the Pharisees, she could have been stoned to death.

The Law of Moses was extreme, thank God for Jesus death that freed us from the bondage of the Law.

During the Law, if a person is caught in adultery, that person would be stoned to death.

The Law was to bring people to their end so that they will look for a savior, thank God for our savior. Jesus Christ. During the Law, there were many offerings that had to be offered and each of these offerings had a blessing attached to it, offerings such as the sin offering, the peace offerings, the burnt offerings, the fellowship offerings, the grain offering, the thanksgiving offering etc. All these offerings typify Christ's sacrifice and were all done in one altar. Jesus fulfilled the Law including these offerings on the cross for us and all the blessings attached to it are now ours.

John 1:17 "for the Law was given by Moses, but grace and truth came by Jesus Christ."

The Law was given, grace came, do you see any difference. The Law was not a person, grace is a person, the Law was given from afar, Grace is near to us in the person of Jesus Christ. Grace brought relationship the Law could not. The Law had glory but grace has greater glory, the Law made us conscious of sin, grace makes us conscious of God's love, the Law was given by a servant, grace came by Jesus, the Son. The Law was a ministry of death (in the sense that many people died under the Law)

2 Corinthians 3:7-8 "Now if the ministry of death, chiseled (engraved) in letters of stones, came with glory, so that the sons of Israel were not able to look directly as Moses' face because of the glory from his face – a fading glory – how will the ministry of the Spirit not be more glorious.

2 Corinthians 3:9 "for if the ministry of condemnation (the Law) had glory, the ministry of righteousness overflows with even more glory".

During the Law, the seal of being a child of God was circumcision but during grace, the seal that we are children of God is the Holy Spirit in us.

Ephesians 4:30 "And grieve not the Holy Spirit of God, whereby you are sealed unto the day of redemption. We were sealed with the Holy Spirit when we believed in Jesus (accepted Him into our lives).

Romans 8:1 "The (Holy Spirit) Himself testifies (bears witness) together with our spirit that we are God's children."

At the time of Jesus, there were four (4) festivals and I will show you why it's very important to note this. The four (4) festivals are the Passover festival, the festival of unleavened bread, the festival of first fruits and the Pentecost.

The festivals of the Passover and the unleavened bread are blended together. The festival of unleavened bread is for seven (7) days and the first day of the unleavened bread is the Passover festival.

The festival of first fruits is when the Israelites bring their first harvest of their crops to the High priest in the temple (Exodus 23:16-20). The festival of Pentecost is done 50 days after the Passover. The Law was given 50 days after the first Passover.

Now read carefully, Jesus died on the festival of Passover, He was buried during the festival on unleavened bread, He resurrected on the festival of first fruits and the Holy Spirit came down on the day of Pentecost (Acts 2:1-4). The Holy Spirit came down on the day of Pentecost which was 50 days after the Passover.

Let's talk about the festival of first fruits for a Moment.

Leviticus 23:9-12[9]And the LORD spoke to Moses, saying,[10]Speak to the children of Israel, and say to them, When you come into the land which I give to you, and shall reap the harvest thereof, then you shall bring a sheaf of the first-fruits of your harvest to the priest:[11]And he shall wave the sheaf before the LORD, to be accepted for you: on the morrow after the sabbath the priest shall wave it.[12]And you shall offer that day when you wave the sheaf an he lamb without blemish

of the first year for a burnt offering to the LORD.

Leviticus 23:15 "And you shall count from the day after the Sabbath, from the day that you brought the sheaf of the wave offering, seven Sabbath; (seven full weeks) shall they be".

In summary, the Israelites will bring their first fruits of their lands produce bring it to the priest who waves it to God for a greater harvest. Jesus fulfilled this festival,

The Bible referred to Jesus as the first fruit.

1 Corinthians 15:20-23[20] But now is Christ risen from the dead, and become the first-fruits of them that slept.[21]For since by man came death, by man came also the resurrection of the dead.[22]For as in Adam all die, even so in Christ shall all be made alive.[23]But every man in his own order: Christ the first-fruits; afterward they that are Christ's at his coming.

Jesus is the first fruit that gave birth to a harvest of the family of God (believers of Christ). When Jesus resurrected, He was yet to ascend to heaven (as the waving of the first fruits) to God.

John 20:17[17] Jesus saith unto her, Touch me not; for I am not yet ascended to my Father: but go to my brethren, and say unto them, I ascend unto my Father, and your Father; and to my God, and your God.

James 1 :18 "And it was of His (God's) own free will that

He gave us birth (as sons) by (His) word of Truth, so that we should be a kind of first fruit of His creatures (a sample of what He created to be consecrated to Himself).”

The resurrection of Jesus as the first fruits gave birth to new creatures. The Ark of Noah which was a shadow of Jesus Christ. It came to rest on the day of first fruits. When the Ark rested and it's occupants were out, that pictured God bringing new creatures to the earth. Noah was like a new Adam and his children filled the earth.

We are new creatures because of the sacrifice of Jesus on the cross of Calvary. Since Jesus, the real first fruits has come and fulfilled the old testament first fruits, don't let anyone tell you that first fruits is about giving things; no it's about Jesus.

12 DISPENSATIONS

So many Christians have no idea about this topic, they may have heard of it but they do not know what it truly means that's why their Christianity is in a circle. And they continue to get God wrong.

Dispensation is defined as a period of time in which God deals (or relates) with a people concerning a revealed truth. There are four main dispensations,

1. Dispensation before the Law
2. Dispensation of the Law
3. Dispensation of Grace
4. Dispensation of the kingdom

Dispensation before the Law

- Period: From Adam to Moses
- Righteousness: through faith in God
- Judgement : through conscience
- Pioneer: Abraham- Gal. 3:6 "Abraham believed God and it was accounted to him for righteousness

Dispensation of the Law

- Period: From Moses to Jesus Christ
- Righteousness: By the Law- Deuteronomy 6:25 "And it shall be our ROGHTEOUSNESS, if we observe to do all these commandments (Law) before the LORD our God as He hath commanded us, Rom. 9:31, Exo. 20
- Judgement: By the Law

- Pioneer: Moses – John 1:17 "For the Law was given by Moses but grace and truth came by Jesus Christ, Deuteronomy 5:3

Dispensation of Grace

- Period: Christ to date
- Righteousness: Faith in Jesus Christ- Rom. 3:21-22 "But now apart from the Law, God's righteousness has been revealed – attested (witnessed) by the Law and Prophets, that is God's righteousness through faith in Jesus Christ, to all who believe, since there is no distinction

Romans 10: "For is the end of the Law for righteousness to those who believe (faith).

1 Corinthians 1:30 "But from Him you are in Christ Jesus, who for us became wisdom from God, as were as righteousness, sanctification, and redemption" (Rom. 9:31-32).

- Judgement: Jesus Christ – John 3:16 "For God so loved the world, that He gave His only begotten Son (Jesus) that whosoever believe in Him shall not perish but have everlasting life, Acts 17:31.
- Pioneer: Jesus Christ – John 1:17 "For the Law was given through Moses, but grace and truth came through Jesus Christ.

Dispensation of the Kingdom

- Period: The second coming of Christ
- Righteousness: Jesus Christ

- Judgement: Jesus Christ
- Pioneer: Jesus Christ

Some comparisons between Law and grace

- In the Old Testament Christ Jesus is concealed (John 15:1; Gen. 28:12)
- In the New Testament Christ Jesus is revealed. Christ born under the Law Gal 4:4; Luke 2L22-24 but ended the Law Rom 10:4, Eph. 2:15
- In the Law, man initiates, God responds, but in grace, God initiates man responds.
- Grace supplies life – Law demands work
- During the Law, we work for righteousness, during grace, God gives it to us as a gift. The bible said Jesus, the gift of righteousness. In the Old Testament, man had no power over Satan and his forces, under grace we have power over Satan and the demonic.

Inadequacies of the Law

- It had faults – Hebrew 8:7-13; 8:7, For if the first covenant (Law) had been faultless, then should no place have been sought for the second: in other words no need for the second.
- It was temporal – Gal. 3:19
- It could not tackle sin in the flesh Romans 8:3, Colossians 2:16-23
- It could not make its adherers perfect – Heb. 7:18-19; 10:1-12
- No forgiveness to offenders in the Law – Heb. 10:28; 2:2; Deuteronomy 17:2

- It was full of curses. Those who want to keep the Law must obey the whole Law, if not they are cursed. James 2:10; Gal. 3:10; Deuteronomy 27:16
- Those who live by the Law, shall be judged by the Law unfortunately, no flesh could keep the Law. Romans 2:12; Gal. 3:10-12
- The Law of Moses has served its purpose to expose the sinfulness of man and make mankind desire the savior Rom. 7-25.
- The Law had nothing to do with the state of the conscience. Hebrews 9:9

13 THE CROSS

The cross was God's best plan to save man from the power of the devil and reconcile us to Himself through the sacrifice of Jesus Christ His Son.

When man fell, God almighty already had the plan to redeem man and put it under effect. The cross is a big mystery showing God's mighty love and infinite wisdom. That why the devil is hiding this big mystery from God's children bringing in doctrines the apostles never preach; usually creeping in by stealth in the Church hence causing confusion everywhere. God is not the author of confusion.

2 Corinthians 4:3-4 "But even if our Gospel also be hidden (obscured and covered up with a veil that hinders the knowledge of God). It is hidden to those who are perishing and obscured to those who are spiritually dyeing and veiled to those who are lost. For the god of this world has blinded the unbelievers mind (that they should not discern the truth) preventing them from seeing the illuminating light of the Gospel of the glory of Christ (the Messiah) who is the image and likeness of God."

Unfortunately even the eyes of believers have been blinded because they do not hear the cross, they do not know God and man have been reconciled together because of Jesus death.

Romans 5:1[1]Therefore being justified by faith, we have peace with God through our Lord Jesus Christ:

The obedience of the Law doesn't bring Justification. If it did, Jesus wouldn't need to come. Of course God commend good work but that's not brings Justification.

It is sad to see Christians try their best to be accepted by God when they have been already accepted in Christ. There is no amount of good works that can bring that reconciliation. We received the reconciliation for Free and the Jesus overpaid our Sin debt.

Hebrews 9:12 "He went once for ALL into the Holy of Holies (of heaven) not by virtue of the blood of goats and calves, but His own blood, having found and secured a complete redemption.

Let us look at some aspects of the things done for us on the Cross

Galatians 3:13 "Christ purchased our freedom redeeming us from the curse by Himself becoming a curse for us for it is written in the scriptures, cursed is everyone who hangs on a tree" (Deuteronomy 21:23).

Galatians 3:13 "Christ purchased our freedom redeeming us from the curse (doom) of the Law and its condemnation by HIMSELF becoming a curse for us for it is written cursed is anyone who hangs on a tree."

So in order words since Jesus became a curse for us and has redeemed us from the curse of the Law that means all those curses of Deuteronomy 28 and other curses of the Law do not belong to us. We are now left with the blessings that we can stand upon and always claim for ourselves and see results.

Jesus has taken all your curses, but if you are ignorant of the truth the devil will always attack you. So many Christians are still removing curses of forefathers, curses of fore-mothers, curses every Sunday. Since the devil knows you don't know the finished works on the cross, he can still toy with you.

Colossians 2:15 God Disarmed Principalities and powers and made a bold display triumphing over them on the cross."

That means before the cross they were armed but after the cross they are disarmed. So all those witches, wizards, demons, spirit disturbing you have been disarmed you only need to stand on the finished works of Christ.

The devils biggest mess up, biggest fear is the cross that's why he fights so hard to hide this truth even from pastors.

As the roman soldiers were bribed not to tell the truth about Jesus death, so the devil has exchanged the gospel for philosophy, money based teachings, the law, comedy (yes even comedy) enemy must die, my enemies will see me progress teaching, and I prophesy teachings.

Jesus has finished everything that's why He said with a loud voice "IT IS FINISHED" yet we are still trying to finish what has been finished. Since you want to finish what has been finished, then, the finishing will never be finished.

On the cross of Calvary, Jesus wore a crown of thorns on His head, so many don't know the significance of this.

Genesis 3:17-19 "And He said to Adam because you listened to your wife's voice and ate from the tree about which I commanded you, do not eat from it: the ground is cursed because of you, you will eat of it with painful labour all the days of your life. It will produce thorns and thistles for you and you will eat from the plants of the field. You will eat bread by the sweat of your brow until you return to the ground since you are taken from it for you are dust, and returned to the dust."

Jesus wearing that crown of thorns represents the thorns and thistles because after God mentioned the cursed, thorns and thistles followed immediately.

Since Jesus wore that crown on our behalf we are now free from that curse, we can boldly expect and ask God to bless your business, career, finance because it has already been paid for. There is no more painful labour for provision, don't let anybody deceive you saying if you do not sow seed or do this or that you would not prosper you. God will bless the works of your hands.

Satan also used the Law against us; to beat us down, to harm us and envelope us in defeat.

After man fell, the devil had the legal right to cause havoc to mankind but Jesus death has disarmed him., Jesus tore down that legal certificate. Satan not only lacks the right, he also lacks the power if you know your standing

Colossians 2:14 "Having cancelled and blotted out and wiped away the hand writing of the ordinances with its legal decrees and demands which was in force stood against us. This ordinances with its regulations, decrees, and demands. He set aside and cleared completely out of our way by nailing it to the cross. God disarmed principalities and powers that were ranged against us and made a bold display and a public example of the, in triumphing over them on the cross."

These laws can also be traditional laws superstitions, for example in some villages if a person crosses a particular place a very terrible thing might happen to them. The people believe this and it become a law (bond) for them, then if a person crosses that path the village witches, demons will use that law to make something terrible happen to that person.

If you keep praying every week for deliverance and removing ancestral curses the devil will still trouble you because you do not know that deliverance and removal of ancestral curses has been paid for on the cross: your ancestry has been changed from that to Jesus Christ.

Colossians 1:13 "The father has Delivered and drawn us to Himself out of the control and dominion of darkness and has TRANSFERRED us into the kingdom of the Son of His love"

We are not only redeemed but transferred to the Kingdom of God.

Took our sickness

I have heard from many legalistic Christians and teaching that sickness are as the result of sin we are have committed, I am not denying the fact that fornication or adultery can make you contact diseases but even babies, infants, toddlers get sick: Do babies commit adultery? No. we really need to change our belief system towards God and stop seeing Him as a strict old man with a long cane. We need to ask God to show us His heart (love) towards us. Because your belief system determines how you can come to God.

There was a reason why Jesus endured such beatings, such scourge, such torture before He died on the cross. The bible records that no man had suffered like He did on earth. The film passions for Christ does not come close to what Jesus suffered.

Isaiah 53:5 "But He was wounded for our transgressions (sins), He was bruised for our guilt and iniquities, the

chastisement (punishment) NEEDFUL to obtain peace and well being (good health) for us was upon Him (Jesus) and with the stripes that wounded Him you WERE HEALED."

Notice it said " we are healed" it's in past tense it's a done deal for you to be healed. Its a matter of standing on and proclaiming this truth.

One thing I have notice is the relation between forgiveness of sins and healing of diseases. I believe they work hand in hand. That is if you are conscious of your forgiveness you would get your healing.

Psalm 103:3 ...Who (God) forgives every one of all your iniquities, who heals (each one of) all your diseases.

Another instance is in Mathew 9 when Jesus told a paralytic lying on a stretcher was brought to Him. Mathew 9:2 ... **"Have courage son, your sins are forgiven"** what the paralytic man actually needed was healing in that sense but Jesus told him that his sins were forgiven". I believe Jesus was trying to tell us that if we are conscious of His forgiveness, we will receive our healing.

Another verse that suggests what I wrote earlier is

1 Peter 2:24 "He personally bore our sins in His (own) body on the tree (cross) as on an altar and offered Himself on it), that we might die (cease to exist) to sin and live to righteousness. By His wounds you are

healed".

Another door of healing open to us believers is the Holy communion; related to the Passover feast of the Old Testament. When they ate the Passover, they were energized and received the strength needed for their journey.

When Jesus came, He replaced that Passover with the Holy communion.

Let me chip something in. In the eating of the Communion in ancient times, three breads are actually presented on top each other and it is the bread that is at the center that is actually broken and eaten. This signifies the triune God: God the Father, the Son and the Holy Spirit. And it was the Son that came to be broken for us by His suffering as a Man.

Mathew 26:26-28 "Now as they were eating, Jesus took bread and praising God, gave thanks and asked Him (God) to bless it to their use, and when He had broken it, He gave it to the disciples and said, take it this is my body. He took a cup, and when He had given thanks, He gave it to them, saying, drink of it, all of you; for this is my blood of the new Covenant, which (ratifies the agreement and) is being poured out for many for the forgiveness of sins."

When you continue to eat his body (through the bread) you receive healing from sickness and diseases. When you take His blood, you receive life to live above every defeat, proclaiming victory over the devil.

John 6:51-57 "I am the living bread that came down from heaven. If anyone eats of this bread, He will live forever. The bread that I give for the life of the world is My flesh. At that, the Jews argued among themselves, how can this man give us His flesh to eat? So Jesus said to them, I assure you: unless you eat the flesh, of the Son of man and drink His blood, you do not have life in yourselves. Anyone who eats my flesh and drink My blood has eternal life, and I will rise him up on the last day, because my flesh is real food and My blood is real drink. The one who eats My flesh and drink My blood lives in Me, and I in him. Just as the Living Father sent Me and I live because of the Father so the one who feeds on Me will live by Me".

Took our condemnation

I would like to start this with the story of the Samaritan woman, Jesus met by the well. This woman had several husbands, she was probably living in adultery. The Samaritan woman came to the well to fetch at noon at around 12 pm. This is absurd because many women fetched water early in the morning when the water is cool or late evening. So the Samaritan woman might have been avoiding gossips or the condemning words of people.

John 4:6-9 –"Now Jacob's well was there, Jesus therefore being wearied with His journey, sat thus on the well at it was about the sixth hour (12:00pm) when

a Samaritan woman came to draw water, Jesus said to her, "will you give me a drink." Jesus disciples had gone into the town to buy food, the Samaritan woman said to Him, you are a Jew and I am a Samaritan woman. How can you ask Me for a drink? For Jews do not associate with Samaritans".

Jews did not relate with Samaritan because the Samaritans where half Sidonians who worshiped idols and other confrontations they had. So for a Jew to be talking to a Samaritan woman was not normal even to her. Besides aside from being an "unclean person" her morality was in question she was probably a prostitute I would say but Jesus was not bothered. He did not like her being a prostitute but He loved her as a person.

John 4:10-15 "Jesus answered, if you knew the gift of God, and who is saying to you, give Me a drink, you would ask Him, and He would give you living water. Sir you don't even have a bucket, and the well is deep. So where do you get this living water? You are not greater than our father Jacob, are you? He gave us the well and drank from it himself as did his sons and livestock Jesus said, everyone who drink from this water will get thirsty again. But who ever drink from the water that I will give him will become a WELL of water springing up within him for eternal life. Sir the woman said to Him, give me this water so I would not get thirsty and come here and draw water."

John 4:16-18 Go call your husband, He told her and

come back here. I don't have a husband she answered. You have correctly said I don't have a husband Jesus said for you have had five husband and the man you now have is not your husband. What you have said is true. Now Jesus knew this woman was living in sin but did not condemn her instead He commended her for telling the truth to Him, You have correctly said I don't have a husband Jesus said. Jesus telling her the truth about her is trying to send a message to her that I know your flaws but I still accept you."

John 4:21-26 "Jesus told her, believe Me woman, an hour is coming when you will worship the Father neither on this mountain nor in Jerusalem. You Samaritan worship what you do not know. We worship what we do know because salvation is from the Jews. But an hour is coming and now here when the true worshipers will worship the father in spirit and in truth. Yes the father want such people to worship Him. God

is Spirit, and those does who worship Him must worship in spirit and truth. The woman said to Him, I know that the messiah is coming (who is called Christ). When He comes, He will explain everything to us." I am (He), Jesus told her, the One speaking to you."

After Jesus had told her "I AM" referring to Himself as the Messiah. She was absorbing all what has just transpired a moment ago. When she noticed Jesus is the Messiah (the anointed One prophesied), she left her water Jar running to the town.

John 4:28-3-0 "Then the woman left her water Jar, went into the town and told the men, come see a man who told me everything I ever did! Could this be Messiah? They left the town and came to Him."

Let me remind you that it was this same Samaritan woman that came to fetch water at noon so as to avoid people's gossips and condemnation was still the same woman who went out to the town preaching about Jesus to the Samaritan people. And because of her words many in Jesus and were saved. It was God's grace, love and acceptance that changed this person from a woman living in sin to a preacher and Evangelist of the Gospel of Jesus Christ. We can see how people get transformed when the know about God's grace. Who would have thought that kind of a woman would be God's worker. Besides what better way could you spread news at that time without a woman. Jesus' disciples kept urging Him to eat because Jesus should have been tired and hungry when they had left.

John 4:31-34 "in the meantime, the disciples kept urging Him, Rabbi, eat something. But He said I have food to eat that you don't know about. The disciples said to one another, could someone have brought Him something to eat? My food is top do the will of Him who sent Me and to finish His work."

These means it makes God happy when people that are living in Sin comes to Him and then He changes them. As you receive grace from God, God is very happy.

Zacchaeus

LUKE 19:1-2 Jesus entered Jericho and was passing through. And there was a man called by the name of Zacchaeus; he was a chief tax collector and he was rich"

Tax collectors at that time were known to be traitors by the Jews because they worked for the Romans who ruled them, and were also regarded as thieves. Zacchaeus was not only a tax collector but a chief tax collector, which made him an easy target for insults, and condemnation by the Jews.

Luke 19:3-4 "Zacchaeus was trying to see who Jesus was, and was unable because of the crowd, for he was small in stature. So he ran on ahead and climbed up into a sycamore tree in order to see Him, for He was about to pass through that way".

With Zacchaeus actions you would see he actually had a heart for God, he really wanted to see Jesus.

Luke 19:5 "When Jesus came to the place, He looked up and said to him. Zacchaeus, hurry and come down, for today I must stay at your house"

Zacchaeus hearing these words must have excited and surprised him. A man hated by the Jews, a social outcast wanted to visited Jesus.

The people were grumbling, they were not pleased with it. Zacchaeus hurried down and received Him gladly.

This is the only time Jesus told someone to Hurry; hurry to receive Him. Jesus wants mankind to hurry to gain salvation.

John 19:8 "Zacchaeus stopped and said to the Lord (Jesus). 'Behold Lord, half of my possessions I will give to the poor, and if I had defrauded anyone of anything, I will give back four times as much."

Jesus didn't actually tell him to return what he stole but because he saw His grace, he not only returned what he stole, but added to it and even gave to the poor. Because of God's grace, a thief became a giver.

God's grace transformed him, he was not the same. So if God's grace does not change you, you should really check yourself before it's too late.

A historian said that Zacchaeus became a Bishop in a town in Ceasarea.

The woman caught in adultery

John gives an account about the Woman caught in Adultery: brought by the Pharisees in order for them to accuse Jesus.

John 8:2-5 "At dawn He went to the temple complex again, and all the people were coming to Him. He sat down and began to teach them, then the scribes and Pharisees brought a woman caught in Adultery,

making her stand in the center. Teacher, they said to Him, "This woman was caught in the act of committing adultery. In the Law Moses commanded us to stone such women. So what do you say."

Well I don't know much about adultery but I know adultery was an act between a man and a woman why was only the woman brought and since the Law commanded such women to be stoned to death, then why don't they just do it, they brought her to Jesus in order to trap Jesus to have a means to accuse Him.

If Jesus says don't stone her, then the Pharisees would say Jesus is against the Law of Moses but if Jesus says stone her the Pharisees would say where is the forgiveness of sins that Jesus preached.

John 8:6 "they asked this to trap Him, in order that they might have evidence to accuse Him. Jesus stopped down and started writing on the ground with His finger."

Jesus writing on the ground with His finger was a miracle that the Pharisees did not notice because the ground of the temple complex was overlaid with stones and there was no sand there to write on. Jesus writing on a stone with His finger is similar to God writing the ten commandment on two stone tablets.

Exodus 31:18 "When He God had finished speaking with him (Moses) upon Mount Sinai, He gave Moses the two tablets of the testimony, tablets of stone,

Written By The Finger Of God.

Jesus was indirectly telling the Pharisees that I know the Law because I wrote the Law."

John 8:7 "When they (Pharisees) persisted in questioning Him, He stood up and said to them, "The one without sin among you should be the first to throw a stone at her."

Did Jesus condone her sin? No. Did He condemn her? No. However Jesus was the only one without sin yet He did not stone her instead gave her a gift of no condemnation.

Jesus turned His attention to the Pharisees.

John 8:8-10 "Then He stopped down again and continue writing on the ground. When they heard this, they left one by one, starting with the older men. Only He was left with the woman in the center. When Jesus stood up, He said to her. Woman, where are they? Has no one condemned you?"

John 8:11 "No one Lord, she answered "neither do I condemn you, said Jesus Go, and sin no more."

Notice the woman answered Jesus "No one Lord," she called Him Lord. Usually the people who call Jesus 'Lord' believe He is the Son of God but those who usually call Him 'Teacher (Rabbi) don't believe Him as the Son of God. Some that were even close to Jesus did not believe Him as the Son of God. Jesus brothers did not believe in His deity when He was alive. Judas was somebody that followed Jesus, saw miracles yet did not believe Him.

Mathew 26:21-22 "While they were eating, He said, I assure you one of you will betray Me. Deeply distressed, each one began to say to Him, surely not I, Lord. The eleven disciples answered Jesus surely not I Lord but Judas reply was a little different."

Mathew 26:25 "Then Judas, his betrayer replied, surely not I rabbi (Teacher) at that point the eleven called Him Lord"

Judas called Him 'Rabbi'. From the example of Judas, its possible someone can go to church but does not believe in Jesus, and has not accepted Him into their lives. Some refer to Jesus as a prophet. From God example Nicodemus, lastly there are some who refer to Jesus as the Lord and as a Teacher or prophet, example as the disciples' even Zacchaeus referred to Jesus as 'Lord'

Luke 19:8 "But Zacchaeus stood and said to the Lord, Look, I'll give half of my possessions to the poor, Lord! And if I have extorted anything from anyone, I'll pay back four times as much".

It was the 'No condemnation Jesus showed to the adulteress that changed her life. This is the same 'no condemnation' given to us by the death of Jesus on the cross and by His shed blood.

Romans 8:1 "There is therefore No condemnation" to them which are in Christ Jesus, who walk not after the flesh, but after the Spirit.

The Bible said there is "No condemnation" not "No correction" for those in Christ Jesus. God corrects His children because He loves them. God doesn't correct with sickness, death or poverty.

I find it important to add this two contrasting figure. Nicodemus and the Samaritan woman.

John 3 talks about Nicodemus, a religious leader of Israel, a Pharisee, but the next chapter which is John 4 talks about an 'ordinary person'. See how Jesus related with them differently.

Nicodemus was a master theologian, a religious leader, Jesus even called him 'teacher of Israel', He had the Torah (Holy book of the Law) whereas the Samaritan woman was 'ordinary' did not really know much, was not a religious leader, was taken to be unclean.

Nicodemus did not open his heart to receive from Jesus, He did not really believe in Jesus even though he should because the book of the Law prophesied many times about Jesus, but the Samaritan woman did not have the book of the Law but opened her heart to receive from Jesus.

Nicodemus puffed up by his knowledge of the scripture could not grasp the understanding of the Spirit. Jesus seeing he did not open his heart to Him, explained the things of the Spirit in a very complicated way but the Samaritan woman who did not really have scriptural knowledge but opened her heart, Jesus explained the things of the Spirit by using something as simple as water.

Nicodemus came to see Jesus at night because he did not want Pharisees to see them together, but Jesus went to the Samaritan woman at daytime even though it was a taboo for a Jew to relate with a Samaritan.

At the end of their meeting Jesus, the Samaritan woman received from Jesus and went out happy, and even preaching about Him in their cities, but Nicodemus left not receiving anything from Jesus.

Now knowing the scriptures is very good but don't read the scriptures and miss Jesus. God doesn't want us to just have the letters of the Bible in our head, but also the Spirit and the Life.

The Pharisees read the scriptures daily but did not believe Jesus even though the scriptures spoke about Him.

John 5:39-40 "You diligently study the scriptures because you think that by them you posses eternal life. These are the scriptures that testify about Me, yet you refuse to come to Me to have life."

This is the same thing today may of us read the bible yet miss the whole concept of Jesus. Open your heart to see Jesus in His word and the Holy Spirit will show you Jesus.

Took our shame

When Adam fell, by disobeying God and eating from the tree of knowledge of good and evil, he became naked and he hid from God.

Genesis 3:10 and he (Adam) said "I heard you (God) in the garden and I was afraid because I was naked.

Nakedness also means shame, because of shame, Adam hid from God. But praise be to God because Jesus has taken all our shame.

The film passion of Christ and many other films depict Jesus on the cross wearing a cloth around his waist but in reality, Jesus was crucified Naked, taking the shame of man on the cross, so that we would now run to God instead of hiding from Him.

God is displeased at the Church when they do not preach about the finished work of Christ on the cross. Jesus endured the brutal torture and shame on our behalf yet we make light of the cross and don't even preach it. We are preaching other things making the Cross of none effect.

1 Corinthians 1:17[17]For Christ sent me not to baptize, but to preach the gospel: not with wisdom of words, lest the cross of Christ should be made of none effect.

Where the cross is not preached, the Holy Spirit will not manifest.

14 GOD'S REST

Hebrews 4 started with urgency to tell us the magnitude of what is about to be said. It made an analogy between the word preached to the children of Israel concerning the promised land and the Gospel today

Because of their unbelief they did not enter the rest God intended for them. Then it took us back to the creation where God rested from His work of Creation. The promised land was also for rest for the Israelites but the Israelites couldn't enter because of unbelief. That rest of the promised land was only a shadow of the real rest which is the Cross.

Hebrews 4:10[10] For he that is entered into his rest, he also hath ceased from his own works, as God did from His". This verse tells us that God's rest in redemption is the Cross which He also instituted for mankind.

Hebrews 4:11[11]Let us labour therefore to enter into that rest, lest any man fall after the same example of unbelief.

This verse tells us to Labour in this rest (which is the Cross) lest any fall into unbelief (that's to say if our focus is not in the cross of Jesus, we are automatically in unbelief) but when we focus on the cross; verse 12 follows that the word of God will be quick affecting every facet of our Lives.

Hebrews 4:12[12] For the word of God is quick, and powerful, and sharper than any two-edged sword, piercing even to the dividing asunder of soul and spirit, and of the joints and marrow, and is a discerner of the thoughts and intents of the heart.

This is the established formula in this era, this is the primary focus of Christianity: Jesus and Jesus alone.

15 THE 70 WEEKS

God's timetable for the world is Israel. To understand the end time, the best place to look is Israel. Israel is God's end time clock.

In the book of Daniel, Daniel was praying earnestly for his people Israel, he prayed continuously and fervently for God's forgiveness for the people of Israel.

Daniel 9:21-24 "Yes, while I (Daniel) was speaking in prayer, the man Gabriel whom I had seen in the former vision, being caused to fly swiftly, came near to me and touched me about the time of the evening sacrifice. He instructed me and made me understand; he talked with me and said, O Daniel, I am now come forth to give you skill and wisdom and understanding at the beginning of your prayers, the word (giving an answer) went forth, and I have come to tell you, for you are greatly beloved. Therefore consider the matter and understand the vision seventy weeks (of years, or 490 years) are declared upon your people and upon your holy city (Jerusalem), to finish and put an end to transgression, to seal up and make full the measure of sin, to purge away and make expiation, to bring in everlasting righteousness, to seal up (end) vision and prophecy and prophet, and to anoint a Holy of Holies (most Holy)".

A week in the Bible is 7 years not 7 days. Looking at the story of Jacob, after Jacob had worked for Laban 7 years to marry Laban's daughter Rachael; however, Laban tricked Jacob and gave Leah, Rachael's elder sister to Jacob at night. Jacob slept with Leah thinking it was Rachael. When morning came, Jacob realized he was deceived, and confronted Laban.

Genesis 9:26-27 "And Laban said, it is not permitted in our country to give the younger (in marriage) before the elder. Finish the wedding feast) week (for Leah); then we will give you (Rachael) also, and you shall work another seven years (for her)."

This has shown us that 1 week means 7 years.

The angel continued speaking to Daniel.

Daniel 9:25 "know therefore and understand that from the going forth of the commandment to restore and to build Jerusalem until the coming of the Anointed One (Jesus Christ), shall be seven weeks (of years) and sixty two weeks (of years); it shall be built again with city square and moat but in troublous times."

In this verse there are two timings, 7 weeks and 62 weeks; let's start with the 7 weeks, **"From the going forth of the commandment to restore and build Jerusalem until the Anointed one (Jesus Christ) shall be seven weeks of years".**

1 week equal 7 years, therefore 7 weeks equal 7 x 7 years which

is 49 years.

2 Chronicles 36:22-23 "Now in the first year of Cyrus, king of Persia, that the word of the LORD GOD by the mouth of Jeremiah (a prophet) be accomplished, the LORD stirred up the Spirit of Cyrus King of Persia, so that he made a proclamation thought all his kingdom and also put it in writing. Thus says Cyrus King of Persia. All the kingdoms of the earth the LORD, the God of heaven, has given me, and he has charged me to build Him a house (temple) in Jerusalem which is in Judah. Whoever there is among you of all His people, may the Lord his God be with him, and let him go up to Jerusalem."

From when Cyrus gave the command for Israelites to leave Babylon to rebuild the temple to when the temple was rebuilt was exactly 49 years. Since we are done with the first let's look at the second part is 62 weeks.

As we have seen, 1 week equal 7 years, therefore 62 weeks is 62x7 equal 434 years. According to the verse from the time when the temple was rebuilt to when Jesus came and died was 62 weeks (434 years) exactly.

Since we are done with the 7 weeks and the 62 weeks, 1 week still remains to complete 70 weeks, 62 weeks added to 7 weeks is just 69 weeks, so 1 week remains to make it 70 weeks. That 1 week (7 years) was suspended so that we Gentiles can come into the family of God through the believing of Jesus Christ. Before this one week starts, we Christians have been taken up through the rapture.

Daniel 9:27[27]And he shall confirm the covenant with many for one week: and in the midst of the week he shall cause the sacrifice and the oblation to cease, and for the overspreading of abominations he shall make it desolate, even until the consummation, and that determined shall be poured upon the desolate.

In summary the anti-Christ will make a strong covenant with many people (perhaps Israel) so that God's temple would be build but in the middle of the 7 years, which $3^1/_2$ years, the ant-Christ will come into God's temple in Jerusalem and do abominable thing in the temple and place his image on the pinnacle of the temple calling himself God. And after the anti-Christ has done all these God will judge him and he will receive the punishment he deserves.

16 The Sacrifice and The Offerings Of The Old Testament

In the Old Testament, there were a lot of sacrifices and offerings made, these sacrifices usually involves a clean animals (Ram, Lamb, Sheep, Goats, Ox, Bull, Turtle doves). The sacrifice of Ram or other clean animals started from the time of Adam to Noah – to Abraham even to the time of Jesus. These sacrifices follow the offerings in the Bible, the burnt offering, the fellowship offerings, the grain offerings, the thanksgiving offering, the sin offering and the peace offering, guilt offering.

The offerings and sacrifices was a temporary justification towards God that is why it had to be made continually. Anytime a person sins or the whole nation sins, sacrifices are made to purify them. The animal brought must be without defect, must be a clean animal (Ram, Lamb), its bone must not be broken

Numbers 9:12 "They shall leave none of it the Lamb) till morning nor break any bone of it, according to all the statutes for the Passover they shall keep it."

The sacrifice is then passed through the fire and after that the offender is forgiven for his sins. These lambs were only a shadow of Jesus Christ.

When John saw Jesus coming to be Baptist "He said this is the Lamb of God that takes away the sin of the world."

John 1:29 "The next day, John saw Jesus coming to him and said, look! There is the LAMB OF GOD who takes

the sin of the whole world."

The Lamb to be sacrificed was to be without defect or blemish (symbolic for sin) Jesus was without sin. None of the Lamb's bone was to be broken; when Jesus was on the cross none of his bones were broken despite those beatings. Even when Jesus was nailed on the cross none of His bones broke. When the Romans soldiers were asked to break the bones of Jesus, they couldn't do it because Jesus was already dead.

Psalm 34:20 "He (God) keeps all His (Jesus) bones; not one of them is broken.

The offering or sacrifice was to be burnt (symbolic for judgement). Jesus took all of God's fiery judgement on the cross. God judged Jesus ruthlessly because of us because that was needed for our redemption.

Just as the sacrificed Lamb should not be kept till morning as said in

Number 9:12 "They shall leave none of it (Lamb, or the sacrifice) till morning nor break any bone of it; according to all the statutes for the Passover they shall keep it."

The body of Jesus was not left on the cross after His death. His body was carried away because the next day was the Sabbath day and the Sabbath Laws forbids any dead body from still being hung on that day

John 19:30-31 "When He had received the drink, Jesus said it is finished. With that, He bowed His head and gave up His Spirit: Now it was the day of preparation, and the next day was to be a special Sabbath. Because the Jews did not want the bodies left on crosses during the Sabbath, they asked Pilate to have the legs broken and the bodies taken down".

These acts showed us God's intentions without the Jews and the Romans knowing it. With all these explanations, I have shown you why and how the sacrifices and offerings were a shadow of Jesus.

Hebrew 10:1-7 "The law is only a shadow of the good things to come that are coming – not the realities themselves. For this reason it can never by the same sacrifices repeated endlessly year after year make perfect those who draw near to worship. If it could, will they not have stopped being offered? For the worshipers would have cleansed once for all, and would no longer have felt guilty for their sins. But those sacrifices are an annual (continual) reminder of sins, because it is impossible of the blood of bulls and goats to take away sins therefore, when Christ came into the world, He said; sacrifice and offerings you (God) did not desire but a body you prepared for me; with burnt offering and sin offerings you were not pleased. Then I said, Here am I it is written about me in the scroll. I have come to do your will, O God."

The offerings and sacrifice gave a temporary justification. It could not make them perfect, if it could it would have just been offered only once and perfected them. It could not perfect them that's why it was made continually every year.

These sacrifices could only cover sins not take them away. Though it was required by Law as God gave but God was not really pleased with it so God prepared a body for His Son Jesus to be the perfect sacrifices that perfects us. God was not really pleased with the sacrifices and offerings but it was required then allow me to say it was the only option at that period of time. But unlike the sacrifices and offerings of Law which was made regularly and could not perfect the worshipers, Jesus our High priest and our offering made just one sacrifice, and perfected and cleansed forever those who believe.

Hebrew 10:11-14 "And every priest standeth daily ministering and offering regularly the same sacrifices which can never take away sins. But this man (Jesus), after He had offered One sacrifice for sin forever sat down on the right hand of God from henceforth expecting till His enemies become His footstool. For by one offering He hath perfected forever them that are sanctified.

Don't let the devil fool you into thinking God hates you, or God wants nothing to do with you, or God is always looking at you to strike you when you have done wrong.

The High priest always stands because there is no chair to seat on. The priest stands daily ministering and offering: This is God telling us that the sacrificing is a continual thing that's why there was no chair in the temple; hence no rest for the priest for their work is still to go on continually.

Hebrews 10:12[12]But this man, after he had offered one sacrifice for sins for ever, sat down on the right hand of God;

For Jesus who is now our High Priest: to sit down means that His work for redemption, justification, purification, perfection and cleansing of us who believe is finished it is a done deal on the cross. That is why He proclaimed on the cross "IT IS FINISHED".

The earthly priest stands signifying continuation of sacrificing and offering but Jesus but Jesus now our high priest sits; signifying completion.

In the Old Testament after a sacrifice has been made the priest makes sure the fire does not go out (quench). The Bible said Jesus died through the eternal Spirit in a sense as if the Cross doesn't just stay in the past, it's continual.

In the Old Testament the priest and high priest have very similar ministry. The priest are in charge of sacrificing a lamb for an offender. This time it is the offender that brings the Lamb to the priest; While the high priest sacrifices a clean animal for the whole Nation of Israel yearly. The high priest is concerned with the temporary justification of the whole nation and this time it is he who chooses and brings the Lamb; sacrificing it as a guilt offering (burnt offering and sin offering) to the Lord.

When an offender or a guilty person wants to be justified before God he brings the clean animal; the priest then inspects the Lamb to make sure it has the right qualities needed. The guilty (offender) places his hands on the head of the animal symbolic for transferring his guilt (offence) on the animal and the animal transfers its own cleanliness (righteousness) on the guilty hence an exchange. The guilty becomes temporarily justified.

This is exactly what Jesus did on the cross to justify us before God forever. He took away all our sins upon Himself and gave us His Righteousness.

2 Corinthians 5:21 "For our sake He made Christ to be sin who knew no sin, so that in and through Him we might become endued with viewed as being in, the righteousness of God in Christ."

Jesus death on the cross us an exchange a transaction a payment. Many of us think on the cross Jesus was paying the devil; no that notion is horribly wrong, Jesus and the devil had no business together. The bible said that if the demonic had known what Jesus death would bring, then they would not have crucified Jesus.

1 Corinthians 2:8 "None of the rulers of this age or world (Satan's kingdom) perceived and recognized and understood this, for if they had, they would never have crucified the Lord of glory."

Satan had no clue of what God planned and I'm certain that one of the reasons they did not know this because they could not believe God would love mankind so much as to give His only Son for them.

When Adam sinned, mankind forfeited His inheritance, man lost it all. God's righteous judgement was hanging on us. Jesus has brought reconciliation between God and Man.

Romans 5:11 "Not only so, but we also rejoice and exultingly glory in God (in His love and perfection) through our Lord Jesus Christ, through whom we have now received reconciliation."

Even before the Law was given, the sacrificing of the lamb to God was in place. One example is Abel

Genesis 4:3-4 "In the course of time Cain presented some of the Land's produce (fruits, vegetables) as an offering to the Lord and Abel also presented (a sacrifice, an offering) some of the firstborn of his flock and their fat portions. And the Lord had respect and regard for Abel and for his offering but for Cain and his offering He had no respect or regard. So Cain was exceedingly angry and indignant, and he looked sad and depressed."

Why did God accept Abel's sacrifice but not Cain's? Some insinuate that it was because Abel gave God his best offerings even the first born for that matter. But no that's not the reason.

Abel gave God the animal sacrifice which was a picture of Jesus, the Lamb of God that would come and be sacrificed for mankind.

I don't know where Abel had gotten that idea from because the Law was given hundreds of years after. He may have gotten the idea from his father, Adam or by revelation from God and He followed the instructions.

Genesis 3:4 "And Abel also presented a sacrifice (a clean animal offering) of the first born of his flock and their fat portion. And the LORD had respect and regard for Abel and his offering."

The way Abel presented His offering is similar to the way the priest during the Law carried out the sacrifice for justification especially when he brought the fat portions. God had respect and regard for Abel's sacrifice because it was a shadow of Jesus sacrifice on the cross. Cain did not follow the way parents had been doing. God was highly pleased with Abel's sacrifice.

Another example is Noah.

After Noah left the Ark after the flood was over he sacrificed clean animals before God

Genesis 8:20 "And Noah builded an altar unto the Lord and took of every clean beast, and of every clean fowl and offered BURNT OFFERING on the altar to God."

Burnt offering are the most important offering. For Noah to do this after the flood means he was also offering burnt offering before the flood: no wonder He pleased God so much in all the earth at that period. Maybe He learnt it from his father or by revelation from God because the Law was not given yet.

17 The Leviticus and Jesus

The primary aim of the whole Law was not man's obedience but Jesus fulfilment. The law was given with Jesus in mind. It was what Jesus needed to fulfil Ito prove He was the Messiah and was highly qualified to be our Redeemer. The Law gave details of the Messiah; Jesus came to fulfill those details. Jesus was the pin-point fulfilment of Bible prophecy. Though the Law was written in letters; Jesus was actually the Spirit of the Law. No wonder he told the Pharisees that the Law, the Psalms and the prophets talk about Him yet they wouldn't still accept Him.

The book of Leviticus points to certain offerings carried out as commanded by God under the law in the old testament which was fufilled by Jesus on the Cross. The levitical offerings were established to give more details on the then coming perfect offering which was Christ Jesus. Each of these offerings may be similar but still carry specific details that completes what may be seemingly lacking in each of them but Jesus was the fulness of them all. The offerings being.

- ★ The burnt offering
- ★ The meat(or meal) offering
- ★ The Peace offering
- ★ The Sin offering
- ★ The Trespass offering

The altar used for sacrifice was made of bronze in four corners just like the Cross of Jesus, the offering (a clean animal without blemish was used) as Jesus was the only man without blemish(Sin), Fire was used to burn the animal signifying God's judgement on Jesus(the offering).

John 1:29 " The next day John sees Jesus coming to Him and says 'This is the Lamb of God who takes away the Sins of the whole World.

The clean animals used were Bullock's, oxen, lambs, goats, turtle doves but the lamb was usually used. The poor who could not afford Bullock's, oxen or lamb were to bring Turtledoves as Mary the mother of Jesus did. So even the rich and the poor needs sacrifice.

THE BURNT OFFERING:

Leviticus chapter 1 gives details about the Burnt offering. The offerer brings the male lamb to the priest a male lamb without blemish for sacrifice.

Leviticus 1:3-4 " If his offering be a burnt offering (sacrifice) of the herd, let him offer a male (clean animal) without blemish. He shall offer it to the Lord of his own free will at the door of the terbanacle of the congregation before the LORD. And he shall put his hand upon the head of the burnt offering and it shall be accepted for him to make atonement for him.

The offerer brings his offering (the animal) to the priest and lays his hand on the head of the offering signifying in effect the offerer(Sinner) transferring his sins to the animal. The animal is then killed or burnt peculiar to the burnt offering just as we transferred our sins to Jesus on the cross and Him bearing our sins and taking our judgement.

THE MEAT OFFERING:

Also referred to as the Grain offering. This offering in actuality is Thanksgiving offering. In this offering blood was not shed as opposed to the other offering. The meat offering signified the Life of Christ while the burnt offering; His death

Leviticus 2:4 "And if you bring an oblation of a meat offering baked in the oven, it shall be unleavened cakes(symbolic of the sinless nature of Christ) of fine flour (symbolic for the perfect life of Jesus) mingled with oil(which signifies the Holy Spirit) anointed with oil(Jesus was mingled with oil in the sense that He was conceived of the Holy Spirit, anointed with oil was when John saw the Holy Spirit come upon Jesus in form of a dove)

Leviticus 2:8-9 "And you shall bring the meat offering that is made of these things unto the Lord when you shall present it to the priest, he shall bring it to the altar.

And the priest shall take of the meat offering a memorial thereof and shall burn it upon the altar; it's an offering made with fire a sweet savour into the LORD".

The life of Jesus was a sweet savour to the LORD. His Life so pleased the Father even to His death, God said "This is my beloved Son, in whom I am well pleased. We too who believe in Jesus death and resurrection, His Life has been deposited in us and we too are a sweet savour (fragrance) to God. But we need to grow more in that Life by making Jesus our Focus.

THE PEACE OFFERING:

The peace offering also called the fellowship offering was an offering made in order to be at peace with God and continue to fellowship.

Leviticus 3:1-2" And if his oblation be a sacrifice for peace offering, if he offers it of the herd; whether it is a male or a female, he shall offer it without blemish to the LORD. And he shall lay his hand upon the head of his offering and kill it at the door of the terbanacle...

The offerer placing his hands upon the is symbolic for transferring God's anger from himself to the animal which is then put to death hence the anger has been appeased. On the Cross, God's anger and judgement over sin was blasted on His Beloved Son in order for we to be at peace with God.

Colossians 1:20-21 "For God was please to have all His fullness dwell in Him and through His death, reconcile everything into Himself (God) by making Peace through the blood of His Cross whether things on Earth or things In heaven. And you that were sometimes alienated and enemies in your mind by wicked works, yet now has He reconciled to God.

Romans 5:10" For if, when we were enemies, we were reconciled to God by the death of His Son, much more being reconciled we shall be saved by His Life".

2 Corinthians 5:18 "All things are of God, who has reconciled us to Himself and given us the ministry of reconciliation (the Gospel).

THE SIN OFFERING:

The sin offering has the same requirements of all what the burnt offering requires basically; a young Bullock or lamb without blemish is brought to the priest and the offerer (sinner) lays his hands on the offering. But there is a specific difference between the burnt offering and the Sin offering. In the sin offering, the sins of the offerer (sinner) is transferred to the offering (animal) while in the burnt offering the purity(righteousness) of the offering is transferred to the offerer. Did you see the difference?

The two offerings were also fulfilled on the cross by Jesus.

2 Corinthians 5:21" For God made Christ who knew no sin to be sin for us, so that we may be made the righteousness of God in Christ.

There's was an exchange.

THE TRESPASS OFFERING:

Leviticus 5 talks about the trespass offering. In the trespass offering gives more details about the offerings of the rich, the middle class and the poor even the poorest of the poor. The rich could offer a Bullock, the middle class a lamb or goat, and the poor pigeons or turtledoves, the lamb is usually used. Any offering brought to the priest was handled in specific ways but had the same end result. The trespass offering is an offering that comes with a special requirement.

Leviticus 5:16" And if he shall make amends for the harm he has done in the Holy thing and shall add a fifth part to it and give it to the priest and the priest shall make atonement for him with the ram of the trespass offering".

In this offering, if a man sins against God in the Holy thing , he would restore a 120% or if he sins against man, either by deceit or theft, he is to restore 120%(all sins are ultimately against God) thus the one that was offended becomes a gainer. Jesus is our trespass offering. All what God has lost because of Adam sins; His death restored it and added to it, by effect God becomes a gainer. God gained more in redemption than He did in Creation even before Adam's sin. That's how effective Jesus death on the Cross was. But the gain was not only for God alone but also for us. Jesus being the bridge between God and man everything He accomplished affects both parties.

Adams fall as a result of Satan's deceit brought great sorrow to the world. He lost his relationship with God, his dominion over the earth which by default he handed over to Satan that's why the earth is full of chaos and misery. Jesus came on a rescue mission to restore everything man had lost. Jesus our trespass offering not only restored our Spirit hence reconnected us to God but also made us Sons(female inclusive) our position with God was even promote than Adam's (Adam was not a Son).

Galatians 4:4-6 "But when the fulness of time came, God sent forth His Son, made of a woman, made under the Law to redeem them that we're under the Law that we might receive adoption as sons. And because you are Sons, God sent forth the Spirit of His Son into our hearts crying Abba Father.

It doesn't stop there verse 7 goes on to say "Wherefore you are no more a servant but a son and if a son, then an hour of God through Christ Jesus" in other words all what

Jesus has: His righteousness, authority, God's love for Him, His Life is also available to Us and we will receive the Full Inheritance when He comes again but we can walk in them to a degree on earth by knowing Him More.

Since Jesus is still our substitute as He died in God's eyes we died too, as He resurrected we also resurrected and as He is seated at the Right hand of God we are also seated in God's eyes. Jesus is seated at God's right hand as a Man representing us. He isn't there for Himself, He is already God.

The trespass offering also covers for the sins of Ignorance. Even the sins you are not aware of: because no matter how much you confess your sins there are still sins you are not aware of. Jesus as our trespass offering covered all that. His blood atoned for even the minute or smallest detail of sin only God knows about. Jesus on the Cross was our trespass offering. After all the torture, horrible treatment Jesus said

Luke 23:34 " Father forgive them for they do not know(ignorance) what they do....... At this point, Jesus showed Himself as the trespass offering.

It took 5(five) different major offerings to portray what Jesus did on the Cross. He came to fulfill the Law and that He did.

THE YEAR OF JUBILEE

At the time of creation, God used 6 days to fully complete the creation of the whole earth and on the seventh day, He rested (not because He was tired but because creation was complete). Since He rested on the seventh day, He brought Israel into the same practice.

For Six days they are to work and on the seventh day (the sabbath), they are to rest from all their labour. The sabbath day as instructed by God wasn't just weekly but yearly and the grandest of all was to be the year of Jubilee. In the yearly sabbath, after 6 years of work, they are to let the land rest for a year, and In that year of rest, God Himself will bring a bountiful harvest in that period.

Consequently in the later years, Israel went about 490 years ignoring this sabbath year which would total 70 sabbath years that they ignored this commandment from God. Hence the reason why Israel was captured and languished in Babylon 70 years and the land will rest by force. The 70 years that they refused to let the land rest will be recovered in their captivity in Babylon. The book of Daniel gives account of their stay in Babylon. Why did God give so much care to the Land? Because like Israel, He also redeemed the Land too. The land was related to Israel. Remember in the beginning: as Adam fell as a result of Sin, all Creation fell too. And when man is finally and totally redeemed from the Fall, creation will be redeemed too.

The year of Jubilee is basically a compilation of sabbaths (a day of rest) and it became a sabbath of all sabbaths. There was a weekly sabbath, a yearly sabbath and a fiftieth year sabbath.

Leviticus 25:8[8]And you shalt number seven sabbaths of years unto you, seven times seven years; and the space of the seven sabbaths of years shall be unto you forty and nine years.

The fiftieth year sabbath will actually entail two years of sabbatical years in succession. The first one will be a seventh year of the seven year cycle, and the next one would be the fiftieth year, which was the year of Jubilee.

Leviticus 25:9-10[9]Then shalt thou cause the trumpet of the jubilee to sound on the tenth day of the seventh month, in the day of atonement shall ye make the trumpet sound throughout all your land.[10]And ye shall hallow the fiftieth year, and proclaim liberty throughout all the land unto all the inhabitants thereof: it shall be a jubilee unto you; and ye shall return every man unto his possession, and ye shall return every man unto his family.

The year of Jubilee is a very important year in which things start afresh. It coincided with the Day of atonement, where the High Priest enters the Holy of Holies with the blood of a ram to purify the entire nation and receive instructions for that year.

In this year of Jubilee, prisoners were set free, slaves were set free, all debts were cancelled, properties are returned to the original owner and all contracts were voided. It was as if everything came to a restart. It was symbolic of the new beginning which a person experiences when they come to Jesus.

Leviticus 25:12[12]For it is the jubilee; it shall be holy unto you: ye shall eat the increase thereof out of the field.

Because it was holy to God, it should be holy to Israel too because it was symbolic of Christ who was to come and die to set man Free; make things new in the eyes of God.

The Day Of Atonement

The Day of Atonement is one of the most important offerings of the Old testament. A particular day is set apart in an entire year for this offering and the only time when all Israel are required to fast. It is a day when the High Priest goes into the Holy of Holies (the presence of God) to purify all of Israel and to receive instructions from God for the entire year. For us to understand the significance of this celebration we need to go in depth to it.

The terbanacle (or temple) of Israel was made up of three distinct places, each bearing more significance to the Last. It was made up of

- ★ The Outer court
- ★ The Holy Place
- ★ The Holy of Holies

The outer court is where the Israelites stay to offer sacrifices and offerings to God.

The Holy Place is where the Priest makes use of these sacrifices and offerings; where they kill the animals and offer them on the Altar

While the Holy of Holies is specifically reserved for the High Priest who goes there only on the Day of Atonement once a year and with much preparation because his Life literally depends on it.

We are just going to run through the Basics, greater information will be dispensed in the Sequel of this Book.

The Journey of the High Priest to the Holy of Holies starts from the Outer Court, then to the Holy place which was separated from the Holy of Holies by a Curtain.

The outer court contains the Brass altar where the sacrifice of carefully selected Animals are made and their blood obtained.

The Holy place contains the table, the show bread and the Lampstand. It also contains the Laver altar that where the High Priest washes himself as it contains water.

The Holy of Holies - wherein is the mercy seat, the cherubim's, the ark of the covenant, the tablets of the Law, Aaron's Rod that budded, golden censer, golden pot hidden manna; the place where the High Priest enters once a year. On Entry to the Holy of Holies, the High Priest ties a long rope with bells that jingles around his waist incase he misses any of the requirements or makes a mistake hence end up being struck dead and his lifeless body will be drawn out. However if he succeeds, he walks out alive. We should know that it is the purity of the Blood that determines the acceptance of the whole of Israel including the high priest. Not even his position is enough.

Why are all these important? It's because the terbanacle of Moses was just a symbol of the heavenly terbanacle.

Hebrews 8.5 They serve in a place of worship that is only a copy, a shadow of the real one in heaven. For when Moses was getting ready to build the Tabernacle, God gave him this warning: "Be sure that you make everything according to the design I have shown you

here on the mountain."

This terbanacle was only a copy or shadow of the real one in Heaven. And if there's a heavenly terbanacle, there should be a heavenly sacrifice with far much greater effect and a heavenly High priest.

Hebrews 10:19-21[19]Having therefore, brethren, boldness to enter into the holiest by the blood of Jesus,[20]By a new and living way, which he hath consecrated for us, through the veil, that is to say, his flesh;[21]And having an high priest over the house of God;

So for the Heavenly Terbanacle; Jesus is the Sacrifice (whose sinless blood is needed), He is the Veil or curtain separating the Holy place from the Holy of Holies (He needs to be sacrificed first for it to be opened), and He is also the High Priest of the Heavenly Terbanacle. You remember that after Jesus died, the veil of the temple separating the Holy place from the Holy of Holies was torn.

Matthew 27:50-51[50]Jesus, when he had cried again with a loud voice, yielded up the ghost.[51]And, behold, the veil of the temple was rent in twain from the top to the bottom; and the earth did quake, and the rocks rent;

As Jesus died, the Veil of the heavenly terbanacle was removed so much that it reflected on the Earthly terbanacle thereby tearing it from top to bottom; signifying that the presence of God was accessible to all mankind.

Jesus was not only the Veil, He was the sacrifice whose sinless blood was needed.

Hebrews 9: 11-12 Now the Messiah has appeared, high priest of the good things that have come. In the greater and more perfect terbanacle not made with hands (that is, not of this creation), [12] He entered the Holy of Holies once and for all, not by the blood of goats and calves, but by His own blood, having obtained eternal redemption.

Unlike the earthly terbanacle which could only purify the Israelites once in every year, the sacrifice of Jesus was a once for all time sacrifice and for the whole world (but can only be accessed by those who believe in Jesus death and resurrection)

Hebrews 9:24-28[24] For the Messiah did not enter a sanctuary(terbanacle) made with hands[only a mode] of the true one) but into heaven itself, that He will now appear in the Presence of God for us.[25] He did not to this to offer Himself many times, as the high priest enters the sanctuary yearly with the blood of

another.[26] Otherwise, He would have had to suffer many times since the Foundation of the World. But now appeared on time, at the end of the ages, for removal of Sin by the Sacrifice of Himself.[27] And just as it is appointed for people to die once -- and after this, Judgement---[28] so also the Messiah, having been offered once to bear the Sins of Many, will appear a second time, not to bear Sin, but to bring Salvation to those who are waiting for Him.

So we have seen how Jesus is the Veil, the Sacrifice and the High Priest. Anybody that claims they are priests that go to the presence of God for people is clearly not operating according to the Bible but some man-made Traditions.

The Way has been Opened so that all can come.

18 The Triune God

Even though we know the Father, the Son and the Holy Spirit are one, we still think they act apart or have different characters or personality. I went to a church and I heard that of all the TRIUNE, the Holy Spirit was the strictest. And He hated sin the most. Truth be told I thought that it was a very funny thing to say, I was shocked. So many times the bible points out to us that these Three are one. They are one person with different offices. Just as man was created in three parts, the Spirit, Soul and Body; and we were made in God's image.

Isaiah 9:6 "For unto us a child (referring to Jesus) is born, unto us a Son is given and the government shall be on His shoulder and His name shall be called Wonderful, Counsellor, the Might God, the everlasting Father, the prince of peace.

Here Jesus is referred to as the MIGHTY GOD and the everlasting FATHER (GOD THE FATHER).

1 Corinthians 15:45 "so it is written: the first man Adam became a living being, the last Adam (Jesus) became a life – giving SPIRIT (Holy Spirit)."

Here Jesus is referred to as the Holy Spirit.

Colossians 2:8 "See to it that no one carries you off as spoil or makes you yourselves captive by his so-called philosophy and intellectualism and vain deceit (idle fancies and plain nonsense), following human tradition

(men's idea of the material rather than the spiritual word), just crude notions following the rudimentary (basic) and elementary teachings of the universe and disregarding Christ Jesus (the Messiah). For in him (Jesus) the whole fullness of Deity (Godhead) continues to dwell in bodily form (giving complete expression of the Divine Nature)."

Jesus is the fullness of God in the flesh (in the human nature). Anything Jesus did, the healing, the feeding of multitudes, casting out demons, raising the dead, accepting and showing grace to social out casts, sinners was all under the influence of God. God can now relate with mankind through Jesus even though man was unclean.

John Adejoro–Oluwa Author of the Book 'Hearing God's voice' tries to let us know that Jesus came back to us through the Holy Spirit. He writes "When the Lord was here on earth, before He went on to the cross, He led the disciples in everything and they depended on Him wholly for everything. He told them what to do and how to do it. He was available to answer all their questions. They did not need a book or any other thing. All they needed was just Him in their midst. Also, if you read John chapter fourteen carefully, you will discover that the Lord was the One who was to come back in the person of the Holy Spirit. He declared in verse 28… **"I go away, and come back again unto you**…." Same Comforter. He said to them (and to us) that He was coming back in the Person of the Holy Spirit. Earlier in verse 18, He told them "I will not leave you comfortless. I will come to you. Having told them in verse 16 **of "Another**

comforter, that (would) abide with you (the church) forever", He continued in verse 17 **"Even the Spirit of truth; whom the world cannot receive, because it sees him not, neither knows him but ye know Him: for He dwells with you and shall be in you".** If I had been among the disciples who heard Jesus speak, and I was in doubt because I did not know or see the Spirit of Truth He was talking about, I would has asked the Lord, where is He? This is because He said that they know Him, and that He dwells with them and shall be in them. "But for us today, we can readily understand that the Lord Himself was the One with them and would be in them". Now the Lord is that Spirit and where the Spirit of the Lord is, there is liberty (II Corinthians 3:17). The Lord Jesus, Himself also said, "I will not leave you comfortless, I will come to you, "it means He was the same one who was to come. He was already with them, and He said He would come to them. Again in verse 23 the scripture said "Jesus answered and said unto him, if a man love me, he will keep my words: and my Father will love him, if a man love me, he will keep my words; and my Father will love him, and we will come unto him and make our abode with him" Here again it is clear, it was Jesus Christ who was going to come to make His abode (dwelling place) in us, so, when the Lord, after resurrection, went back to the realm of the Spirit He did not give us a book rather He gave us a person to walk with". If you embrace this then you would know that the Holy Spirit is not stricter than Jesus because they are the same people, the same heart of love, the same willingness to help and comfort you.

The Holy-Spirit works more efficiently when Jesus is preached.

In the redemption strategy, God the Father has done His part in bringing the substitute for mans failings, Jesus has done His part for finishing the works on the cross, the Holy Spirit is the one that would help us have the reality and manifestation of what Jesus has finished in our lives.

The Working of the Holy Spirit

The Holy Spirit works only when Jesus perfect work is preached. Hearing the cross purifies your heart and mind from sinfulness.

Acts 10:1-6 "There was a man in caesarea named Cornelius, a centurion of what was called the Italian regiment. He was a devout man and feared God along with His whole household. He did many charitable deeds for people and always prayed to God. At about three (3) in the afternoon, he distinctively saw in a vision an angel of God came in and said to him, Cornelius! Looking intently at him, he became afraid and said, "What is it, Lord? And he (the angel) told him, your prayers and your acts of charity have come up as a memorial offering before God. Now send men to Joppa and call for Simon, who is also named Peter. He is lodging with Simon, a tanner, whose house is by the sea"

If you notice, when the angel came to Cornelius, the angel just gave him only one instruction "send for Peter", Cornelius obeyed and sent two of his servants to look for Peter explaining exactly what had ensued to his servants.

Acts 10:9-16 "The next day, as they were traveling and nearing the city, Peter went up to pray on the housetop at about noon. Then he became hungry and wanted to eat, but while they were preparing something, he went into a visionary state. He saw heaven opened and an object coming down that resembled a large sheet being lowered to the earth by its four Corners in it were all the four footed animals and reptiles of the earth, and the birds of the sky. Then a voice said to him, 'Get up Peter; kill and eat' No Lord! Peter said, for I have never eaten anything common and unclean! Again, a second time, a voice said to him what God has made clean, you must not call common. This happened three times, and then the object was taken up into heaven."

Peter still having some elements of the Law in his thinking. It was the Law of Moses that categorized animals into Clean and unclean animals. But for the mission Peter is going to be taking, those elements of the Law had to be done away with totally and replaced completely with the Spirit. And that the way to salvation is open to all of mankind. This was about to be put into practice with Cornelius and his household.

Peter wasn't clear about what the vision meant. The men who had been sent by Cornelius, having asked directions to Simon's house, stood at the gate.

"They called out asking if Simon, who was also named Peter was lodging (staying) there. While Peter was thinking about the vision, the Spirit told him, three men are looking for you. Get up, go downstairs and accompany them with no doubts at all, because I have sent them."

When Peter met with them they told him everything that Cornelius experienced with the angel, Peter followed them. After Peter's arrival, he narrated all what he experienced with the angel that appeared to him. Then Peter began to preach the Gospel of Jesus

Acts 10:36-46 "He (God) sent the message to the sons of Israel, proclaiming the Good news of peace through Jesus Christ – He is Lord of all. You know the events that took place throughout all Judea, beginning from Galilee after the baptism that John preached, how God anointed Jesus of Nazareth with the Holy Spirit and with power, and how He went about doing good and curing all who were under the tyranny of the devil, because God was with Him. We ourselves are witnesses of everything He did in both the Judean country and in Jerusalem, yet they killed Him by hanging Him on the tree (cross) God raised up this Man (Jesus) on the third day and permitted Him to be seen, not by all the people, but by us, witnesses appointed before hand by God, who ate and drank with Him after He rose from the dead. He commanded us to preach to the people, and to solemnly testify that He is the One appointed by God to be the judge of the living and the dead. All the Prophet testifies about Him and through His name everyone who believes in Him will receive forgiveness of sins. While Peter was still speaking these words, the Holy Spirit came down on all those who heard the message.

If You notice: Cornelius doing good works did not save him, him seeing a vision didn't save him, his seeing an Angel of God did not save him. It was until the preaching of the Gospel and his believing that saved him

As Peter preached the Gospel of Jesus Christ, the Holy Spirit came and started working in the lives of Cornelius and his household. As Jesus was preached, the Holy Spirit started working.

If Peter did not preach the gospel of Jesus Christ and started preaching about the law, wisdom quotes, favour, breakthrough, money, philosophy or even dangers of hell, the Holy Spirit would not work. Preaching Jesus is not by saying the name alone but also what He did on the Cross.

If the cross is not preached, lives cannot be changed. It's because the love of God displayed on the cross is not being preached, the church has many problems. Even if you preach about hell and scare people from sinning, their lives are not still transformed for the better, because after you have scared them about hell, sometime later, they would go back to their sinful ways.

2 Corinthians 3:18 "We all, with unveiled faces, are reflecting the glory of the Lord and are being transformed into the same image from glory to glory, this is from the Lord who is the Spirit".

The only time the Holy Spirit moves is when Jesus is being preached. So many of us are not seeing miracles and transformations because Jesus is not being preached. The only business the Holy Spirit has is to testify of Jesus Christ.

John 15:25 "But When The Comforter (counselor, helper, advocate), intercessor, strengthener, stand by) Comes, whom I will send to you for the Father, the

Spirit of truth who comes (proceeds) from the Father, He (Himself) will testify regarding me (Jesus)".

The whole Bible talks about one person and that is Jesus Christ. He's the central focus of the Bible.

THE MINISTRY OF THE HOLY SPIRIT

We are now in the Dispensation of the Holy Spirit, this part of the Godhead which is on the move now. For Him to come to the world and be resident, Jesus had to first die before He can be released to the world.

Of the part of the Godhead, the Holy Spirit is in charge of restoration process, right from creation, to Jesus death, and He will set the stage for the second coming of Jesus.

I was reading Psalms 23 one day and a revelation came to me. In that small chapter I saw God the Father, the Son and the Spirit.

From the sentence "The LORD is my shepherd" spoke about God the Father.

Psalms 23:4[4]Yea, though I walk through the valley of the shadow of death, I will fear no evil: for thou art with me; thy rod and thy staff they comfort me.

When I read about the rod, my mind was transported to Moses rod which became the rod of God when the red sea was parted; and that rod was a symbol of the Cross of

Jesus Christ.

Psalms 23:5[5]Thou preparest a table before me in the presence of mine enemies: thou anointest my head with oil; my cup runneth over.

Oil in the old testament signified the Spirit of the Lord, it was used to anoint Kings, Priests and also for sacrifices. After reading the phrase "My cup runs over" I realized that not only will the cup be filled, it will run over. The oil not only fills the cup, it runs over; hence a restoration with an extra.

It was then I realized that the Holy Spirit was in charge of restoration, then I started seeing the pattern and was led to creation. And the Holy Spirit was first mentioned when the eath was referred to. So it seems to be that He was there to set the stage of the restoration of the Earth, which may also imply that the earth in particular was re-created. However this topic is for another day, I may delve more on this in the Sequel of this book.

The Ministry of the Holy Spirit to the world are categorized into three.

John 16:7-8[7]Nevertheless I tell you the truth; It is expedient for you that I go away: for if I go not away, the Comforter will not come unto you; but if I depart, I will send him unto you. [8]And when he is come, he will

reprove the world of sin, and of righteousness, and of judgment:

The Greek word for reprove is 'Elegcho' which means to convict-convince. So He is going to convict-convince the world of Sin, Righteousness and Judgement.

John 16:9-11[9]Of sin, because they believe not on me; [10]Of righteousness, because I go to my Father, and ye see me no more; [11]Of judgment, because the prince of this world is judged.

Of these three categories we are going to look at the one where the Holy Spirit reproves the World of Sin. We would see why He is very important even to the sinful and unbelieving world hence making it easier for them to believe because as we have seen many times in the Bible: signs, wonders and even Judgement cannot convict unbelieving men to believe God. Such examples are the Philistines, the Egyptians, Benhadad (King of Syria), Nebuchadnezzar, Balak, the town where Jesus drove demons into pigs, the Pharisees and more. We'll look deeper into a few.

The Philistines and the Ark Of God.

1 Samuel 4:1-2[1] And the word of Samuel came to all Israel. Now Israel went out against the Philistines to battle, and pitched beside Ebenezer: and the Philistines

pitched in Aphek. [2]And the Philistines put themselves in array against Israel: and when they joined battle, Israel was smitten before the Philistines: and they slew of the army in the field about four thousand men.

The Israelites set out to do Battle against the Philistines without consulting God first. The first phrase "And the word of Samuel came to all Israel" makes it seem like it was God's instruction to battle: but rather it's supposed to be the conclusion of the last verse of the previous chapter. Besides if it was God's instructions, why would they lose so horribly?

1 Samuel 4:3[3]And when the people were come into the camp, the elders of Israel said, Wherefore hath the LORD smitten us to day before the Philistines? Let us fetch the ark of the covenant of the LORD out of Shiloh unto us, that, when it cometh among us, it may save us out of the hand of our enemies.

Not only that they didn't consult God before going for battle, they also didn't consult Him as regarding the bringing of the Ark to the Scene (which was their own idea). After totally neglecting God but still bringing the Ark to the Scene that by default became Idolatry. The Ark of God was now reduced to some magical ornament that brings blessings. To add salt to injury, the Ark was accompanied by the two most evil priests Israel had known which were Hophni and Phinehas.

To cut the story short, despite bringing the Ark, God allowed the Philistines to inflict more Punishment to the Israelites in Tremendous Fashion; so much that the Ark of God which Israel had turned into an Idol was captured by the Philistines, brought into their City called "Ashdod" and ultimately to the house of their god; "Dagon". They thought it was Dagon that got them victory over Israel and their God. They were up for a very big unpleasant surprise.

1 Samuel 5:3-4[3]And when they of Ashdod arose early on the morrow, behold, Dagon was fallen upon his face to the earth before the ark of the LORD. And they took Dagon, and set him in his place again.[4]And when they arose early on the morrow morning, behold, Dagon was fallen upon his face to the ground before the ark of the LORD; and the head of Dagon and both the palms of his hands were cut off upon the threshold; only the stump of Dagon was left to him.

In essence God was showing them that their god Dagon was entirely nothing before Him.

Don't you think common sense or simple Logic should make them Abandon their god and follow the God of Israel since He had utterly destroyed Dagon? Apparently, no amount of wonders or Judgement can change people whose heart has chosen to be stubborn.

One day I randomly asked an Atheist/Agnostic (I don't know where he stands) that " If there was a book that had 2,001 prophecies; 2000 of prophecies were fulfilled won't it be logical to believe that the remaining 1 would be fulfilled? Won't that book be considered divine? Because he liked to say that the Bible is just a normal book written by men and liked to talk about Logic over faith. I asked this question randomly without a context or from where I was coming from. However, he gave me an interesting answer: "He said of course he would trust such a book and believe it to be divine" then I stopped the chat then and took a mental note of what had just transpired. I almost couldn't believe my ears. He then asked where I was coming from but I changed the topic. You'll have to wonder why then wouldn't he believe the Bible that had over 1,817 prophecies fulfilled and still counting. I've told people before; one of the facet of the Bible that can strengthen a believer's faith and counter an atheist or agnostic is through the many prophecies fulfilled in scripture. More would be said concerning this in the sequel of this book.

1 Samuel 5:6-7[6]But the hand of the LORD was heavy upon them of Ashdod, and he destroyed them, and smote them with emerods, even Ashdod and the coasts thereof.[7]And when the men of Ashdod saw that it was so, they said, The ark of the God of Israel shall not abide

with us: for his hand is sore upon us, and upon Dagon our god.

God's judgement wasn't only against Dagon but now against the People. If common sense was to be considered, they should have acknowledged Israel's God and asked for Mercy but rather chose to take the Ark of God to another City called Gath. Their foolishness made them think a change of cities would pause the Judgement. They took the ark to other cities but had the same results.

1 Samuel 6:1-2[1]And the ark of the LORD was in the country of the Philistines seven months.[2]And the Philistines called for the priests and the diviners, saying, What shall we do to the ark of the LORD? tell us wherewith we shall send it to his place.

It's Amazing how they knew this was the Work of God and still won't believe Him and ask for Mercy. Instead, they decided to send the Ark of God away. After taking counsel to send the Ark of God away and how they think it was right to send it, Dagon's priests and diviners said something remarkable.

1 Samuel 6:[6]Wherefore then do ye harden your hearts, as the Egyptians and Pharaoh hardened their hearts? when he had wrought wonderfully among them, did they not let the people go, and they departed?

Not only did they realize this was the Hand of God, they also referenced the Egyptians who because of their stubbornness refusing to let Israel go was met with tremendous consequences. They knew all these yet they didn't follow God and chose to stick with their gods, just as other nations heard of this story. It's amazing all these wonderful miracles of God was shown to man, they admit is the God of Israel but would still decide to follow their false gods.

Nebuchadnezzar

Nebuchadnezzar was a very prominent figure in the ancient times. He was probably the King of the Entire world of his day. His native Kingdom Babylon was the greatest empire of all time; capturing cities, Kingdoms and other empires including Israel.

However it was with the capturing of Israel that He got to know about the God of Israel. Will He come to not only know but serve him? We will find out.

King Nebuchadnezzar had a dream that greatly troubled him and he needed to have an interpreter to explain the dreams to him. However to be sure that his astrologers, magicians and wise men don't just say something out of a figment of imagination or truisms, he asked them to first tell him what he dreamt and the interpretation else they and their families will be killed and their houses ruined.

There was panic in the land because of this decree and it was told to Daniel; a young Hebrew boy taken captive into Babylon. Daniel requested that time be given to him so he can interpret the dream.

Daniel 2:16-18[16]Then Daniel went in, and desired of the king that he would give him time, and that he would shew the king the interpretation.[17]Then Daniel went to his house, and made the thing known to Hananiah, Mishael, and Azariah, his companions:[18]That they would desire mercies of the God of heaven concerning this secret; that Daniel and his fellows should not perish with the rest of the wise men of Babylon.

After praying to God for the revelation of the dream, it was revealed to him.

Daniel 2:19[19] Then was the secret revealed unto Daniel in a night vision. Then Daniel blessed the God of heaven.

Daniel introduced God to king Nebuchadnezzar and told him the dream and it's interpretation. Nebuchadnezzar marveled so much that he fell face down to worship Daniel and gave Glory to God.

Daniel 2:46-47[46]Then the king Nebuchadnezzar fell upon his face, and worshipped Daniel, and commanded

that they should offer an oblation and sweet odours unto him.[47]The king answered unto Daniel, and said, Of a truth it is, that your God is a God of gods, and a Lord of kings, and a revealer of secrets, seeing thou couldest reveal this secret.

Nebuchadnezzar admits that the God of Daniel is the greatest God at least in the revealing of secrets. But would this admission make him actually serve the LORD? No. The very next chapter which is about a decade later, Nebuchadnezzar made a golden statue and orders that the nations of the world serve it else they will be thrown into a furnace of fire. This was a man who had admitted that the God of Israel is the greatest God. This shows the stubbornness of man's heart that even a wonder like this couldn't make him converted.

Shedrach, Meshach and Abednego; three Hebrew boys who were Daniel's companions disobeyed this instructions citing that they couldn't serve other gods; even so much as dismissing the king's threat and trusted in God's ability to save them. They had already sealed their fate; death was not an issue.

The furnace was heated seven times; so hot that those that carried them into it were consumed. Nebuchadnezzar saw something terrifying, three men were put there but he saw a fourth man.

Daniel 3:24-26[24]Then Nebuchadnezzar the king was astonied, and rose up in haste, and spake, and said unto his counsellors, Did not we cast three men bound into the midst of the fire? They answered and said unto the king, True, O king.[25]He answered and said, Lo, I see four men loose, walking in the midst of the fire, and they have no hurt; and the form of the fourth is like the Son of God.[26]Then Nebuchadnezzar came near to the mouth of the burning fiery furnace, and spake, and said, Shadrach, Meshach, and Abednego, ye servants of the most high God, come forth, and come hither. Then Shadrach, Meshach, and Abednego, came forth of the midst of the fire.

Nebuchadnezzar saw a fourth man in the fire which looked like a Son of God (this was a pre-incarnate appearance of Jesus). But not only was there a fourth man, nothing was burnt on these three men, not their clothes or hair they didn't even smell like smoke. Nebuchadnezzar here again acknowledges God and orders that the nations serve God.

King Nebuchadnezzar had another dream about a huge and glorious tree which was cut down to only a stump. Daniel interpreted the dream to the king that he was that great tree which was cut down and whose mind was turned into a beast and drove out to dwell with beast with the intent that he will truly glorify God and that God rules over the kingdom of men. However he wouldn't be cut down entirely hence the stump. A simple condition was given to him to avert this impending doom for him but as we shall see, he brushed it away and just a year later, Nebuchadnezzar became even more proud.

Daniel 4:30-31[30]The king spake, and said, Is not this great Babylon, that I have built for the house of the kingdom by the might of my power, and for the honour of my majesty?[31]While the word was in the king's mouth, there fell a voice from heaven, saying, O king Nebuchadnezzar, to thee it is spoken; The kingdom is departed from thee.

The divine sentence was carried out on Nebuchadnezzar; he was given the mind of a beast and his kingdom was taken from him.

Daniel 4:33[33]The same hour was the thing fulfilled upon Nebuchadnezzar: and he was driven from men, and did eat grass as oxen, and his body was wet with the dew of heaven, till his hairs were grown like eagles' feathers, and his nails like birds' claws.

After a period of seven years, the divine sentence was fully served and Nebuchadnezzar's mind and his kingdom was restored to him and this time it seems he truly acknowledged God. Did Nebuchadnezzar go back to his old ways? It seems not but with his track record we can't be a hundred percent sure.

The advantage of the Holy Spirit to the World.

This two examples of a nation and an individual shows that wonders and judgement has not been effective in converting man; hence the need for the Holy Spirit to the unsaved world. The Spirit goes out to people to convince them about Jesus. But there's still willpower; it can be accepted or rejected. When you submit to His persuasion, He then convicts your heart. The Holy Spirit has been very effective. On the very first day, He was introduced to the world on the day of Pentecost, 3000 people were saved and at another time, 5000 people were saved and still counting even to this day and in the future. The added advantage is that His persuasion is not a one time thing, He can keep His persuasion even to death. But if there's death after rejecting Jesus, there's eternal consequence. So much that imagination doesn't even cut it.

19 Faith and Works

God's first plan in dealing with man was not the law; it was by the belief system but the Israelites asked for the law.

God used the belief system to relate with so many people even in the Old Testament with the likes of Rahab, Ruth, the Gibeonites and even some Gitites that followed David and the mixed-multitude that came out of Egypt with the Israelites.

The notable time God used faith to relate was through Adam as astonishing as this may sound its true. God was the first to preach the gospel (the good news of Christ Jesus) to Adam.

Genesis 3:15 "I will put hostility between you and the woman and between your seed and ser seed He will strike your head and you will strike His heel."

The seed of the woman refers to Jesus because one reason the seed is singular (definite, 1 seed), and biologically speaking women don't have seed, but the woman which is Mary had seed it was implanted in her. So that the virgin birth of Jesus could be possible.

After God had said to the devil about the seed in Genesis 3:15, Adam and Eve believed. What is the gospel? It is the good which ultimately is the gospel. Adam and Eve believed. Previously God said in

Genesis 2:17 "But you must not eat from the tree of knowledge of good and evil for on the day you eat it you will surely die" but in Genesis 3:20 **"Adam name his wife Eve because she was the mother of all living."**

How can Adam possibly name his wife mother of all living which is what Eve means when God had said "The moment you eat of this Tree you shall die"

Adam and Eve believed that the human race will continue because of the news (Gospel) of the seed which is Jesus. Since God saw that Adam believed the Gospel of the Seed (Jesus) God made clothing of skin and of hides because Adam and Eve were wearing leaves.

Genesis 3:21 "The Lord God made clothing out of skins for Adam and his wife, and He clothed them."

God clothed Adam and Eve Himself with Hides and skin of Lamb for a person to get hides and skin from an animal the animal had to be killed first. So God was the first to kill a Lamb and clothed Adam and Eve with the skin. A symbol of God sacrificing Jesus (the Lamb of God) on the cross and clothing us with Jesus righteousness. This is what happens when you truly believe the Gospel. God clothes you with Jesus righteousness.

After the created race fell through Adam, God inaugurated the called race through Abraham. Abraham and his wife Sarah had no children of their own and were well passed the age of child bearing. Abraham was so frustrated, he submitted to the idea that another become his heir. But God had a plan.

Genesis 15:5-6[5]And he brought him forth abroad, and said, Look now toward heaven, and tell the stars, if thou be able to number them: and he said unto him, So shall thy seed be.[6]And he believed in the LORD; and he counted it to him for righteousness.

What is so special about Abraham believing this very words God spoke to Him? This particular seed God is talking about is Jesus Christ.

Galatians 3:16 "Now the promises were spoken to Abraham and his Seed. He God did not say and to seeds as though referring to many but AND TO Your Seed referring to one, Who Is Christ Jesus."

So in simpler terms just like Adam, God preached the news (Gospel) about the Seed and as Abraham Believed this news, it was credited to him as righteousness.

Galatians 15:6" And he (Abraham) believed God and He counted it to him as righteousness."

In essence because Abraham believed in the gospel about the Seed, Abraham became righteous just as we today have become righteous because we truly believe in Jesus Christ. God gave Abraham further instructions

Genesis 15:9 "So the Lord said to him bring me a heifer, a goat and ram each three (3) years old, along with a turtle dove and a young Pigeon."

The animals brought (i.e the heifer, goat, ram, turtle dove and Pigeon) were used for the main offerings to God and we're all shadows of Jesus in context of the offering.

Abraham cut all these animals in pieces on the altar and arranged the halves opposite each other but did not cut the birds. Abraham fell into a deep sleep and a thick dreadful darkness fell on Abraham then God prophesied Israel's slavery in Egypt.

Something even more remarkable happened.

Genesis 15:17 "When the sun had set and darkness had fallen, a smoking fire pot and a blazing torch appeared and passed between the pieces"

And the fire ultimately burning them which symbolizes Jesus Christ. As God's fire passed between these pieces, the same way God's fiery judgement was passed on Jesus Christ on our behalf.

Genesis 17:6 "And I (God) will establish my covenant between Me and thee and thy Seed (singular) after you in their generations for an EVERLASTING covenant to be a God to you and to your Seed after you."

Galatians 3:16 "Now the promise was made to Abraham and his seed. He did not say seeds as though referring to many but "AND TO YOUR SEED" referring to one who is Christ Jesus."

God also used the belief system to relate to many gentiles. Why the belief of the gospel of Jesus Christ could work for both Adam and Abraham even though Jesus did not come to die at those times is because Jesus was crucified since the foundation of the world. God anticipated man's rebellion in the garden and made a solution for him in Jesus Christ His Son.

1 Peter 1:18-20 "For you know that you were redeemed from your empty way of life inherited from the fathers, not with perishable things like silver or gold, but with the precious blood of Christ, like that of a Lamb without defect or blemish. He (Jesus) was Destined before the foundation of the world but was revealed at the end of the times for you."

Revelation 13:8 "And all that dwell upon the earth shall worship Him, whose names are not written in the book of life of the lamb slain from the foundation of the world."

Man's fall brought serious repercussions. He was separated from God his creator because of sin. For Adam to still legally be accepted by God perfectly they had to be a substitute. God loved man so much, but God was still a judge. God makes the rules yet God subjects Himself to His own rules. The bible says "God honours His word more than His name." God always wanted to have intimate relationship with man but man's fall prevented that because God's judgement was hanging on us Hence the importance of a substitute.

2 Corinthians 5:18-19 "And all things are of God, who

hath reconciled us to Himself by Jesus Christ, and hath given us the ministry of reconciliation (Gospel) to with, That God Was In Christ Reconciling THE World To Himself, not imputing their trespasses unto them, and hath committed unto us the word of reconciliation."

"God was in Christ" and reconciling the world to Himself." That means God has been working on earth through Christ His Son to restore that intimacy lost in the Garden of Eden as a result of Adam's fall. Besides it was God planning to go back to man not the other way round.

When God asked Adam where he was after his rebellion was not because God did not know where Adam was but because God was reaching out.

The death of Jesus on the cross has brought us reconciliation. The cross is the ultimate expression of God's love and God's wisdom.

On the cross of Calvary God killed two big birds with one stone. God proved He was unshakable, the unwavering judge and extreme lover of man.

Because of God's immeasurable love to mankind, He blasted all of His brutal judgement on Jesus Christ so that we won't face that judgement at all. Satan was disarmed, rendered powerless and was made a public disgrace because of God's wisdom on the cross of Calvary. You are accepted in the beloved because of Jesus sacrifice on the cross.

God used the faith system to bring gentiles to Himself before the cross so the cross will make it complete.

Rahab:

Rahab was a prostitute in Jericho, her house was directly connected with the awesome walls of Jericho.

The book of Joshua chapter 2 talks about how Joshua sent spies to scout the land of Jericho. They went and came into an prostitutes house called Rahab and lodged there. The king of Jericho asked Rahab about the spies. She lied and misled the king's envoy and hid the spies on her roof in a stalk of flax. After misleading the king of Jericho's envoy she said these to the Israelite spies.

Joshua 2:9-11 "And Rahab said unto the men, I know that the Lord hath given you the Land and that your terror is fallen upon us and that all the inhabitants of the land faint because of you for we have heard how the Lord dried up the water of the red sea for you, when ye came out of Egypt, and what He did to the two kings of the Amorites that were on the other side Jordan, Sihon and Og, whom ye utterly destroyed and as soon as we heard these things, our hearts did melt, neither did there remain any one courage in any man because of you, for the Lord your God, He is God in heaven above and on earth beneath."

Jericho was the most idolatrous city of the Amorites. Rahab's house was part of the wall of Jericho. Rahab was a very popular harlot that even the king of Jericho knew her. Her house was a tourist attraction to so many men.

The people of Jericho heard God dried up the Red Sea and destroyed the two Amorites kings. But from the time God dried up the Red Sea to their moment was over a hundred years so Rahab might have been hearing those stories from when she was little, she has been believing in the true God ever since because she proclaimed to the spies "The LORD your God is God in heaven and on earth".

Rahab was in an idolatrous land yet she had faith in the God of Israel. Though many of the people in Jericho heard these same stories it was only Rahab that believed in God.

At that time anybody that had heard of God's judgement or seen His Power, should Logically believe Him as the true God. But as we have seen especially with Israel no amount of Judgement or miracles can change the state of a stubborn heart; a reason why thc coming of the Holy Spirit is especially advantageous to the world: To help us believe.

If the people of Jericho had believed after hearing those stories they would have stopped their wicked idolatrous ways.

Rahab took a risk hiding those spies. If she had been caught, she and even her family would have been put to death.

Rahab enjoyed a lot of God's grace because of her faith.

Hebrews 11:21 "By faith, the harlot Rahab perished not with them that believed not, when she had received the spies with peace."

God does not commend her deception but He commends her faith. Rahab said to the spies

Joshua 2:12-18 "Now please swear to me by the Lord (she trusted God keeps His word) that you will also show kindness to my family because I showed kindness to you. Give me a sure sign. That you will spear the lives of my father, mother, brothers, sisters and all that belong to them. And save us from death. The men answered her (we will give our lives for yours). If you don't report our mission, we will show kindness and faithfulness to you when the Lord gives us the land, then Rahab let them down by a rope through the window, since she lived in a house that was built into the wall of the city, go to the hill country so that the men pursuing you wont find you she said to them hide yourselves there for three days until they return afterwards go on your way, the men said to her, we will be free from this oath you made us to swear unless when we enter the land, you tie this scarlet (red) cord (rope) to the window through which you let us down. Bring your father, your mother, brothers and all your fathers family into your house if anyone goes out of the door of your house, his blood will be on his own head. But if anyone with you should be hammed, his blood

will be on our heads."

Joshua 2:21 "Let it be as you say, she replied and she sent them away. After they had gone, she tied the scarlet cord to the window."

There is something peculiar about this scarlet or red rope. The scarlet rope in this case represents the blood of Jesus; similar to the blood placed on the door post of the Israelites during their exodus from Egypt.

Exodus 12:13 the blood will be a sign for you on the houses where you are, when I see the blood, I will pass over you. No destructive plaque will touch you when I stroke Egypt."

The spies assured Rahab that scarlet rope hanging on her window will save her. And she believed the words of the spies. So in a way she believed in the blood of Jesus to save her from damnation.

The scarlet rope signifies the blood of Jesus. Even if the whole Jericho had entered the house with the scarlet rope they would have been saved. But even if Rahab had left that house with the scarlet robe she would have been killed.

After the whole agreement between Rahab and the spies, Rahab waited for the promise to be fulfilled. She may have invited alot of people to come in to the house. When the time for Israel to destroy Jericho came, a miracle happened.

When the Israelites had completed their walk round about Jericho's great walls, they sounded the trumpet made with Ram's horn. Then the walls of Jericho collapsed but Rahab's house that was directly part of the building did not collapse because of the scarlet rope. She and any in that particular house were saved. The same way the blood of the Passover lamb saved those inside from God's judgement.

We have also been shielded from God's judgement because of our faith in Jesus Christ.

God was not done with Rahab just yet; she got the most valuable gift ever, she was part of the Lineage that would bring about Christ in His incarnation as a Man. She became the wife of Salmon; one of the spies gave birth to Boaz; husband of Ruth who gave birth to Obed, then Obed begat Jesse, Jesse begat David, and down to Jesus Christ (see Mathew 1:5).

Here we see how merciful God is He used a woman with Zero morality, He did not care about her past, God did not place condemnation on her instead He used her and placed her among the lineage of God's beloved Jesus Christ. Don't think God cannot use you because of your past. Don't you let the condemning eyes of the world stop you from receiving Jesus and from coming to God

Romans 8:1 "therefore there is now no condemnation for those who are in Christ Jesus."

God's grace shown to Rahab worked transformation in her life and her family. She left her idolatrous living to be identified with the people of God, she abandoned prostitution and got married to Salmon a well respected man of Israel. God's love towards her transformed her so well that she was considered a heroine in the bible.

God wants the world to come to know about His loving grace so He can transform them for the better. God is love. Jesus death on the cross is the ultimate representation of God's love and all who believe in Him will be saved (John 3:16). So don't let the devil tell lies that God does not want you because of your past. You are highly accepted in the in Christ. Christ is the means not you.

Ruth

The book of Ruth tells us about an interesting story about Ruth who was a gentile being grafted into the family of God. But this story sinks deeper than what meets the eye. It shows a beautiful picture of how Jesus redeemed us and made us His Bride.

There was a particular tradition in the Jewish custom called "Kinsman Redemption". Based on this tradition, when a Jew dies or becomes bankrupt and in the process losses all his properties, a Kinsman Redeemer (that the person to redeem the bankrupt Jew) which is a relative and usually of higher financial standing can buy back what was forfeited of the bankrupt Jew and also inheriting his responsibilities to his Wife if he had no Son. The Kinsman

Redeemer is usually the closest relative to the dead or bankrupt Jew. If he refuses to redeem it, he can transfer the rights to another less close relative.

Naomi and her family left the land of Israel because of poverty (famine), she left to Moab and settled there with her husband's and her two sons who later married Moabite women.

Ruth 1:1-5" During the time of the judges, there was famine in the Land. A man left Bethlehem in Judah with his wife and two sons. The man's name was Elimelech and his wife's name was Naomi. The names of his two sons were Mahlon and Chillion. There were from Bethlehem Ephratah in Judah. They entered the Land of Moab and settled there. Naomi's husband died and she was left with two sons. Her son's took Moabite women as their wives; one was named Orpah and the second Ruth. After they lived in Moab for about 10 years, both Mahlon and Chillion also died, and Naomi was left without her two children and without her husband".

Naomi lost everything and decided to return back to Israel because the famine has ceased. Ruth had made up her mind to follow Naomi to Israel and worship God.

Naomi had a kinsman of her husband's side, a prominent man of wealth called Boaz who heard about Naomi's plight and Ruth's honourable actions. Boaz commended

Ruth for her actions towards her mother in-law and how she left her people to come to a people she didn't know before. Boaz favored Ruth and showed concern for her. Ruth reported to Naomi all that Boaz told her and how he showed her favor. Naomi then filled in the blank spaces and gave Ruth instructions on what to do in order to get Boaz to be her Kinsman Redeemer which Boaz gladly accepted. But there was already a closer kinsman than Boaz.

When the day for the kinsman redemption came, Boaz went up to the gate and sat there and kinsman whom Boaz spoke about came (the one who was a close kinsman to Naomi) to whom he asked to sit down In the presence of the Elders as witnesses..

Ruth 4:3-10" And Boaz said to the Kinsman, Naomi who came back from Moab has determined to sell a parcel of land which was our brother (relative) Elimelech, I thought I should inform you: Buy it back in the presence of those seated here and In the presence of the elders of the people. If you want to redeem it, do so. But if you don't want to redeem it tell me because there is none before you to redeem it and I am next to you ' I want to redeem it he answered'. Then Boaz said, on the day you buy the Land from Naomi, you would also marry Ruth the Moabitess, the wife of the dead man to raise up the dead upon his inheritance (that is if a Son is born from

this marriage union, the son would inherit the redeemed Land). The kinsman replied ' I can't redeem it by myself, or I will ruin my own inheritance. Take my right of redemption because I can't redeem it'. Now this is the manner of the former time a man removed his sandal and gave it to the other party in order to make any party legally binding concerning the right of redemption or the exchange of property. This was the method of legally binding a transaction in Israel so the Kinsman his sandal and said to Boaz 'Buy back the property yourself'. Boaz said to the elders and all the people ' You are my witnesses today I have bought all that was Elimelech's and all that was Chillion and Mahlon's of the hand of Naomi. Moreover Ruth the Moabitess, the wife of Marlon have I purchased to be my Wife to raise up name of the dead upon his inheritance, that the name of the dead be not cut off from among his family and from the gate of his place(because they wrote their genealogies at the gate) you are witnesses today. So Boaz redeemed the properties and Married Ruth.

As I have pointed out before. The Bible talks about one person Jesus Christ from Genesis to Revelation in types and symbols it's the Spirit that can reveal that to us.

How does this story of Ruth relate to Jesus? Boaz was a symbol of Jesus Christ. Since Boaz was a kinsman (relative). Jesus also became man's Kinsman (Relative) by becoming a Man Himself.

John 1:14" And the WORD (Jesus) became flesh (man) and Dwelt among us...

Mankind lost everything because of Adam's, we forfeited everything including our authority, Creation and our Spirits were dead (disconnected from God) and became slaves to Satan because of sin. No man could redeem us except Jesus (our heavenly Boaz) because He was the only one without sin. He didn't have the sin tainted blood line of Adam and was the only one qualified. Ruth on the other hand who was a gentile which were not in the family of God but were to be redeemed and grafted in.

But the closer kinsman which was symbolic of the Law couldn't redeem us, it could only point out our problems but offered no solution whatsoever.

Galatians 3:23-24" Before this Faith (Jesus) came, we were confined under the Law imprisoned until the coming Faith was revealed. The law then was our master our guardian UNTIL Jesus Christ so that we could be Justified by faith.

The closer kinsman symbolic of the Law couldn't redeem us (the law only showed man his faults but offered no solution) so the Law had to give way for Jesus who alone could redeem us.

Galatians 4: 4-5 "But when the completion of time came, God sent His Son (Jesus) born of a woman, born under the Law to REDEEM those under the Law so that we can receive adoption as Sons.

Since the Law couldn't redeem, Jesus took it up for us and paid with His own Blood (death on the Cross) bringing back our relationship with God, saving us from hell and Satan and restoration of our high standing with God(Jesus is seated at the right hand of God in the heavens as Man's representative, He is already God). Jesus has restored man to an even higher standing with God even before Adam's fall. The whole of Creation would be fully restored at the end.

Boaz not only redeemed Ruth but also married her, she was his bride. We too are the Bride of Christ.

Romans 7:4 "Wherefore my brethren, you also are become dead to the Law by the Crucified body of Christ that you should be married to another even to Him who is raised from the dead that we should bring forth fruit to God.

As Ruth 4:10 shows the kinsman redemption was also used to raise up name for the dead so that the name of the dead would not be cut off from the people. So in a sense the dead man can continue to live through the Son born from this union. How does this relate to Jesus?

Colossians 2:13"And when you were DEAD in sins and in the uncircumcision of your Flesh, HE made you alive with Him(Jesus) and forgave all our trespasses".

This tells us that since Jesus is our substitute, that as He died, in the Eyes of God we also died and as He resurrected, we also resurrected from the dead. This is the premise of us being new creatures.

True Faith results in works.

Paul in His account in Romans makes a case for Faith above works telling us that we are justified by faith and not by what we do; citing an example with Abraham, the circumcision and the Sacrifice of Isaac. James however seems to make a case for works but the misconception we have is that Paul and James made contradictions on this Faith and works issue both citing Abraham. But the true issue is that as Paul wrote that Faith is Paramount, James makes the case that True Faith should produce good works by default. That Faith and good works should not be separated. Works follow faith but faith does not follow works. We should realize that the true definition of faith is Jesus and what He did on the Cross. With these highlighted points, we can now proceed.

James 1:22-24[22]But be ye doers of the word, and not hearers only, deceiving your own selves.[23]For if any be a hearer of the word, and not a doer, he is like unto a man beholding his natural face in a glass:[24]For he beholdeth himself, and goeth his way, and straightway forgetteth what manner of man he was.

This verse try to bring in the importance of works which is the doing part of that verse. As I have said James isn't putting works over faith rather he is putting works as a result of Faith in it's primary definition. He used an example of a man who looks at a mirror and forgets what he looked like just a few minutes after. In essence James is saying true faith will actually produce good works (right believing will result to right living). So how can we be doers of the word and not just hearers?

James 1:25[25]But whoso looks into the perfect law of liberty, and continues therein, he being not a forgetful hearer, but a doer of the work, this man shall be blessed in his deed.

So the way we become doers of the word is by looking at the **perfect law of liberty** (which is the Jesus and what He did on the Cross) and Continue (emphasis on continuing). Its an active focus on the cross in your focus (your study, prayer, meditation, then you will become to act accordingly.

2 Corinthians 3:18[18]But we all, with open face beholding as in a glass the glory of the Lord, are changed into the same image from glory to glory, even as by the Spirit of the Lord.

It is our consistent looking at the Lord (Jesus and what He did on the Cross) that's how we are being changed to His image). The more you consistently behold the more you are like Him, the less you behold, the less you be like Him. It's not rocket science. It is these works that are the results of our consistent beholding that is referred to as "Fruits".

Galatians 5:22-23[22] But the fruit of the Spirit is love, joy, peace, long-suffering, gentleness, goodness, faith,[23]Meekness, temperance: against such there is no law.

But if there are "fruits" there should also be a tree and that tree is the Cross of Calvary

1 Peter 2:24[24] Who his own self bare our sins in his own body on the tree, that we, being dead to sins, should live unto righteousness: by whose stripes ye were healed.

And who was on that tree that bore our sins and by whose stripes we are healed? Easy; it's Jesus (John 15:1-6)

John 15:5[5]I am the vine, ye are the branches: He that abides in me, and I in him, the same brings forth much fruit: for without me ye can do nothing.

If you notice it said Abide some translations use remain: not visit. When you abide in the vine you bear fruit. We can see here that true Faith (in Jesus and what He did on the Cross) will produce good works as James tries to make that point. Right Believing will result to right Living.

20 Seeing Jesus in the Bible

In Luke 24:13-35 – the disciples of Jesus were on the road to Emmaus they talked to themselves about Jesus Christ who was crucified. When they were talking to themselves Jesus join them on the road and talked to them but Jesus made them not to recognize Him. They told Jesus that Mary and the rest went to the tomb where Jesus body was laid but could not find the body but saw angel that told them Jesus was alive. Jesus answered them

Luke 24:25-27 "He Jesus said to the how unwise and slow you are to believe in your heart all that the prophets have spoken, did not the Messiah have to suffer these things and enter into His glory then beginning with Moses and all the prophets, He (Jesus) interpreted for them the things concerning Himself in all scriptures."

So Jesus started showing them Himself in the scriptures, how the Law and the prophets talked about Him and finally

Luke 24:30 it was as He (reclined) at the table with them, He took bread, blessed and broke it and gave it to them. Then they knew it was Jesus.

Jesus did not want them to recognize Him physically but wanted them to see Him in the scriptures. Today Jesus wants us to see Him in His word (the bible) and it's the Holy Spirit that can help you see Jesus in the Bible so ask Him.

Do you know why it's importance to Focus on Christ and see Him in the Word?

2 Corinthians 3:18[18]But we all, with open face beholding as in a glass the glory of the Lord, are changed into the same image from glory to glory, even as by the Spirit of the Lord.

The more you focus on Christ, the more you will be like Him. The less you focus on Christ, the less you will see like Him.

Let me use this opportunity to talk about addictions as Addictions has been the silent bane of the Church.

So many people especially the youths and teens are suffering from some type of Addictions. A staggering statistics has been giving of Christians especially millennials who are suffering from Pornography addictions alone and even pastors. This is not a means to shame anybody but to shine the light on this rampaging menace.

The Porn industry generates hundreds of millions of dollars annually n and their target audience are kids and teenagers. So they get exposed to porn as early as nine years and usually gets hooked and they grow up with a brain connection that establishes this habit. They can be hooked for years to come; some for months to as long as over Forty years.

However we are not going to talk more about the Problem, we are going to talk about the best Solution which is Jesus.

The more you focus on Jesus, the more you spend time in His Word seeing Him, the more you confess your gift of righteousness in Christ, the more that addiction begins to wane; immediately or gradually losing its grip on you. Not just addictions but other habits, other wrong lifestyles controlling your Life.

Romans 6:14[14] For sin shall not have dominion over you: for ye are not under the law, but under grace.

The Cross of Jesus Christ is the Solution to the Sin problem. Not just in the Spiritual realm but also in our everyday Life.

Some might just be little bad habits, however there are some people who are very comfortable with this situation. Some have been trying to stop it by their will power but nothing seems to work they make promises to God they won't do it anymore but they fail and feel like God is coming to get them. They are enveloped in heavy self- condemnation and the devil uses this opportunity to accuse them to themselves but thank Jesus there is hope, for because of Jesus death

Romans 8:1 "There is therefore no condemnation for those in Christ Jesus…."

God is not condemning you: He want you to come to Him for help.

Anytime you engage in such habits, confess your identity in Christ Jesus, and proclaim the cross. The bible says "the righteousness of faith speaks.

2 Corinthians 4:3 "We having the same Spirit of faith, according as it is written, I believe, and therefore have I SPOKEN; we also believe and therefore I SPEAK." Anytime the urges come confess your identity in Christ.

2 Corinthians 5:21 "For He (God) hath made Him (Jesus) to be sin for us, who knew no sin, that we might be made the righteousness of God" always confess (speak) "I am the righteousness of God in Christ" in the midst of that addiction.

Romans 6:14 "For sin shall not have dominion over you; for you are not under the Law but under grace."

Ask the Holy Spirit to help you walk in the manifestation of how Jesus has freed you from all sorts of bondage on the cross. "He transferred us from the kingdom of darkness, into the kingdom of His beloved Son Jesus Christ. Jesus has already freed you on the cross of calvary through His death. Proclaim the cross and let the Holy

Spirit do the rest..

21 The Two Men (Adams)

The human race is made up of descendants of the two Adams.

1 Corinthians 15:45-49 "And so it is written, the first man Adam became a living being. The last Adam became a life giving Spirit. However, the spiritual is not first, but the natural, and afterward the spiritual. The first man was of the earth, made of dust; the second man is the Lord from heaven. As was the man of dust, so also are those who are made of dust; and as is the heavenly man, so also are those who are heavenly. And as we have borne the image of the man of dust, we shall also bear the image of the heavenly man."

Spiritually there are two men in existence. The billions of human beings on earth are grouped into two. The Bible called them "the first man and the second man". The first man, who was the first created physical man is Adam, while the second man created physically and called the last Adam is Jesus the Lord. Every human being is in either of these men. They are the heads of the Old creation and new creation respectively. As a human being, you are either in the Old creation in the first man Adam or in the new creation in the second man, the last Adam, Jesus the Lord. Now let's look at the features or achievement of these two men and what they mean to us.

FIRST MAN – First man ADAM was made a living soul, naturally, earthly.

OUR (OLD) ANCESTOR

Brought all of us into:

- Sin slavery **(Gen. 2:17; 3:15-24)**
- Death slavery **(Gen. 2:17)**
- Satan slavery
- World slavery **(I John 2:15-17, James 4:4)**
- Brought separation between us and God **(Gen. 3:23-24)**
- Satanic enslavement and afflictions **(John 10:10a)**
- Made us naked (shame) **(Gen. 3:7)**
- Made us slaves to fear **(Gen. 3:7-11)**
- Made us slave to sin
- We inherited curses **(Gen. 3:17)**
- We inherited sorrows **(Gen. 3:16)**
- Incurable death
- After the fall, the first man was inferior to sin and Satan, that was why he could be enslaved by them (Satan was older, became stronger, wiser than him) **Gen. 3:1-13**
- In the first man, we were in bondage to Satan
- In the first man, we were under guilt and condemnation **(2 Cor. 3:7-9)**
- We are born sinners, **Romans 3:23; 5:17-19)**
- Every unbeliever (those that don't believe in Jesus) has the first man as his/her ancestor
- The first man is our natural identity

Transferring from the first man to the second man. Every human being born by the first original man Adam is automatically in the first man and is subject to all the features on the table concerning the first man. There was no solution within the first man of all the woes he caused for himself. That is why God gave (brought in) the second man. The second man was given purposely as solution to the problem of the first man. If there was solution within the first man, God would not have given the second man. Therefore, stop looking at yourself for solution to your problems. There is NONE. The solution is in the second man (Jesus). Outside the second Adam, man is helpless. No religion or philosophy has solution to problem of sin caused by the first man.

Second Man – The second, the last Adam was made a LIFE – GIVING SPIRIT, SPIRITUAL, HEAVENLY OUR NEW ANCESTOR (2 Cor. 5:21) "Therefore if any person is in Christ (the Messiah) he is a new creation (a new creature altogether); the Old (previous moral and spiritual condition) has passed away. Behold, the fresh and new has come).

The second Adam (Jesus) redeemed (freed) us from –

- SIN SLAVERY **(Romans 8:3; 6:6-14)**
- DEATH SLAVERY **(2 Timothy 1:10; Heb. 2:25)**
- SATAN SLAVERY **(Heb. 2:14-15)**
- WORLD SLAVERY **(Gal. 6:14)**
- Reconciled men to God by His death **(Romans 5:9-10)**
- Delivered us from the power of darkness **(Col. 1:13; 2:14-15)**
- Clothed us and bore our shame **(Romans 10:11, Heb. 12:2)**
- Gave us boldness **(Eph. 3:12; 2 Tim. 1:7)**
- Gave us liberty from sin **(Romans 6:14; 5:1; Gal. 3:12)**

- Brought us blessings, took away our curses **(Eph. 1:3; Gal. 3:13-14)**
- He took our sorrow and gave us liberty – blessing **(Gal. 5:1; Eph. 1:3)**
- He took our death (spiritual) and gave us life **(John 3:16; 10:10b; 5:24)**
- The second man is superior to sin and Satan, He could not be deceived and enslaved by them (He was stronger, wiser and older than Satan)
- In the second man we are already delivered on the cross once and for all**. Col. 1:13**
- In the second man, we are forgive and justified. **Romans 5:1**
- We are born righteous – **Romans 5:17-19**
- Every believer is born again and is in the New Man as our ancestor.
- The second man is our new identity – **2 Corinthians 5:17**

The Transfer

Colossians 1:13 "He has delivered us from the power of darkness and conveyed (transferred) us into the kingdom of the Son of His love."

New Birth

To move from the first man to the second man as portrayed in the table 2 is simply to move from death to life. Just as we came into the first man by natural birth, so we come into the second man by birth, the new birth

John 3:3-6 "Jesus answered and said to him, most

assuredly, I say to you, unless one is born again, he cannot see the kingdom of God. Nicodemus said to Him, how can a man be born when he is old? Can he enter a second time into his mother's womb and be born? Jesus answered, most assuredly, I say to you, unless one is born of water and the spirit, he cannot enter the kingdom of God"

John 1:12-13 "But as many as received Him (Jesus), to them He gave the right to become children of God. To those who believe in His name; who were born, not of blood, nor of the will of the flesh, nor of the will of man but of God."

When you receive the good news of the solution to your sin problem and the salvation secured and offered to your sin problem and the salvation secured and offered to us in Christ Jesus, believing in Him with your heart that He died for you and rose again the third day and confessing Him with your mouth as Lord and savior – you are saved.

Romans 10:9-10 "Because if you acknowledge and confess with your lips that Jesus is Lord and in your hear believe (adhere to, trust in, and rely on the truth) that God raised Him from the dead, you will be saved for with the heart a person believes and so is justified (declares openly and speaks out freely and confirms his salvation."

This is the first step in the transfer process from the first man to the second man.

The second step to the transfer is baptism by immersion. Mark 16:16 says "those who believe and are baptized shall be saved." After believing comes baptism. Baptism in the bible is only by immersion in water at all times and interpretation.

Romans. 6:3-4 "Or do you not know that as many of us as were baptized into Christ Jesus were baptized into His death? Therefore we were buried with Him through baptism into death? Therefore as Christ was raised from the dead by the glory of the father, even so we also should walk in newness of life."

Baptism is the practical demonstration of our participation or experience of our death, burial and resurrection with Christ. it is our open and declared identification with the death, burial and resurrection of Christ Jesus, which all the host of heaven and earth cannot deny. At baptism, the transfer from the first man to the second man is undeniably sealed and all the terms of the new covenant delivered to us. Can you imagine what pharaoh and his army would have done to the Israelites if they had not crossed the red sea? He would have brought them back to bondage. That is what it is when a saved one is not baptized by immersion. Though saved but has not crossed the red sea. You know crossing the red sea was a kind of baptism to the Israelites.

1 Corinthians10:1-2 "Moreover, brethren, I do not want you to be unaware that all our fathers were under the cloud, all passed through the sea, all were baptized into

Moses in the cloud and in the sea, all drank the same spiritual drink. For they drank of that Spiritual Rock that FOLLOWED them and that Rock was Christ."

That was what sealed their transfer from Egyptian bondage to liberty and guaranteed the good land they were promised. When you have believed or saved by being born again and are baptized by immersion, then you can now say as Paul said in

We are now new creatures, old things are passed away. Thank God.

Colossians 1:13 "He has delivered us from the power of darkness and conveyed (transferred) us into the kingdom of the Son of His love."

Jesus did not deliver us from us from the power or influence of the power of darkness and left us there to be warring (fighting) in the dark with those forces. No, He transferred, conveyed or translated us to His own kingdom. If you have been delivered and transferred to the kingdom of God's dear Son and you are now in the second man, who is binding (holding you hostage) that makes you go for deliverance every time? It is a question you must answer with the Spirit of Truth in the light of the finished works on the cross. Remember, it is the Truth one knows that sets free (John 8:32)

Breaking Curses

Which of the curses are you breaking, the same ones Christ has carried for you on the cross or fresh ones? Which of your ancestral curses are you breaking, your old ancestor Adam where you have been transferred from the old to your new ancestor Christ where you are now. The devil has blinded the minds of people to the light of the glorious gospel.

You are now in the second man (Adam)

If you have **not** been born again, even if you bear a Christian you are still in the first man, all his features will not be absent from your life. And if you are born again but have not been baptized by immersion you are not completely free from the features of the old man although you are still saved from eternal sufferings in hell. But your transfer is still processing and not yet complete. But if you are saved, baptized by immersion and baptized in the Holy Spirit you are now in the second man. You have nothing to do with the first old man spiritually. You have been transferred; your **new identity** is in the second Adam. Study every detail of this new identity by meditation and prayer. Keep believing and declaring your new identity in Christ with thanksgiving to God for all that Christ has done for you. The devil fears the people who understand what Jesus did on the cross. Let the Spirit of truth shine the light of the truth of the gospel in your heart (2 Cor. 4:3-4 ,6) so that the veil and chains of religion and ignorance can fall of your soul.

What does a substitute mean? A substitute is a replacement of someone or something in the place of another. So on the cross Jesus took your place, He did **not** just die for you, He died as you, He took your sins from you and transferred His righteousness to you. It was a transfer, a trade. Most of Jesus works and actions on earth were an example for us believers to follow.

After man fell to sin in the garden, there was nothing man could offer God of himself to please God, everything man could give to God was detestable because sin infected us.

During the Law any body discharge would make a person unclean be it tears, spit or others would make you unclean, that's how bad it was then. Man lost the glory of God he was clothed with and became naked but thanks to the cross of Calvary. God has clothed us with the Righteousness of His Son making us highly accepted in the beloved.

OUR REPRESENTATIVE

In the Garden Adam was our representation. As Adam was created, all of mankind was created, time just brought us out. That's why as one man sinned he led us into the bondage of sin: we all inherited that sin nature, it was in our bloodline.

As Adam sinned He was stripped of everything, the glory of God that was his covering was gone and he became naked. Man was brought down to the very low, He forfeited it by falling in sin. But God had a plan to restore man and give him even more. He sent His Son Jesus as a complete man, Jesus is complete God and perfect man. He was God in the flesh. Jesus acted in full capacity as a man; He emptied Himself of Divinity.

Philippians 2:7[7]But made himself of no reputation, and took upon him the form of a servant, and was made

in the likeness of men:

That's why the Pharisees could not believe He was the Messiah. They were expecting an illustrious person, shining white and inflicting horror against the enemies of Israel. They were looking for a political Messiah.

God's heart does not only reach out to Israel but to the whole world.

All of Jesus actions was inspired by the Holy Spirit. He followed the Spirit perfectly. On the cross Jesus was our substitute, He died on the cross to confer that same son-ship He had to us.

Jesus is seated at God's right hand not as God, but as man; Man's representative.

Just as Adam was man's representative, Jesus is now our representative. Heaven finally has found a perfect man those under this man are now perfect because of Him.

Romans 6:3-6 "Or are you unaware that all of us who were baptized into Christ Jesus were baptized into His death? Therefore we were buried with Him by baptism into death, in order that, just as Christ was raised from the dead by the glory, so we too may walk in a New way of life. For if we have been joined with Him in the likeness of His death, we will certainly also live in the likeness of His resurrection."

Romans 6:8 "For we know that our old self was

crucified with Him in order that sin's dominion over the body may be abolished, so we may no longer be enslaved to sin, since a person who has died is freed from sins claims.

Our old self that likes to do wrong, that is under sins dominion, under sickness dominion, enemy of God, a prey to Satan has been crucified, its dead, since our self is dead, we now have a new self

2 Corinthians 5:17 "Therefore if any man be in Christ, He is a new creature, old things are passed away behold all things have become new"

Jesus is an example of that New creature we have become, creature that is not under the control of the demonic, a creature where the Holy Spirit dwells in, a creature that does not like to do wrong.

Many people think God wants to see Jesus in us just by our good morals or well behavior ; but God also wants to see us working in authority like Jesus, in casting out demons, healing the sick, raising the dead.

Preaching the gospel along with signs and wonders, He wants to see us exhibit wisdom, He wants to see us relate closely with Him as Jesus, He wants to see us reaching out to the world as Jesus did, He wants to see you prosper and bold as Jesus was. God wants to see us worry free as His Son, He wants to see us free from addictions, bad habits as Jesus was, God wants us to have Wisdom as Jesus did, He wants to see us healthy as Jesus was, He wants to see us use our authority over demons and obstacles as Jesus did and many more.

We get all these as our focus remains on Jesus and what He did on the Cross. Don't let religion hide other things from you, don't let it make you think God only wants you to have good morals alone. That's just part of the fruits of the Spirit.

Epilogue

The writing of this book took approximately three years. Years of Bible reading and revelation. It sets out to not only reach out to the World but also the Church. It covers so many areas from prophecy, warning, instructions, patters and God's formula and at the same time countering some non-biblical interpretations and traditions. It may even give Atheists and agnostics a lot of things to ponder upon.

With the culture and society increasingly becoming hostile to God, people may have started to lose their faith, the concept of God and Christianity has been made to look like a myth or some archaic tradition. This book is made to bring us back into perspective and to show the world that the Bible is actually Divine and can be Trusted.

My dream is for this book to become a big instrument of God to turn many people to himself be it in Africa, Europe , Asia , the Americas , Australia and Antarctica; in villages, cities even in the Forests or deserts .You too can help in this dream by sharing to as much people as you can.

Thanks for reading and God bless you.

ABOUT THE AUTHOR

DaudU, Emmanuel Solomon is just a man with a Burden placed by God to bring the Church back into perspective of its original mandate, to strengthen the belief in the God of the Bible in a world of ever increasing hostility against God and to spread the world about Jesus who God sent to die for the sins of the World

www.ingramcontent.com/pod-product-compliance
Lightning Source LLC
LaVergne TN
LVHW091311150826
845673LV00006B/1611

9798844255960